VIGIL
CANADA'S SACRIFICE IN AFGHANISTAN

Author and Designer
Rod A. McLeod

Researcher and Editor
Norman Leach

Foreword
General (Ret) Rick Hillier

Afterword
Lieutenant-General Stuart Beare

SHELLDRAKE PUBLISHING CO., LTD.
CALGARY, AB, CANADA

This book is dedicated
to the men, women and families
of our Canadian Armed Forces
without whom we would not be able to enjoy
the privileges, rights and freedoms
that Canada has to offer
and to those who gave the ultimate sacrifice...
...and their families who so deeply deserve
our continued respect and support.

FOREWORD

In October 2003. I was selected as the Commander of the NATO-led International Security Assistance Force (ISAF) in Kabul, Afghanistan. As a soldier, it is the kind of task that you both look forward to - and think hard about.

I knew that the job the Canadian Forces was being asked to do was an important one. The United States and all Western countries, had been attacked on September 11th, 2001 and it had been a tough blow. Thousands had been killed and those who supported the attackers had been given sanctuary in Afghanistan.

To remove the threat to the West and to change the lives of the common Afghan, is tough. Decisions and actions had to be taken. No one thought it would be easy – and it wasn't.

That said, I also knew that I was leading the best sailors, soldiers and airmen/women in the world – The Canadian Forces. We were part of a coalition of NATO and other Allies and, ultimately, ANA and ANP. Together with these forces, Canada was in the right place to make a real difference.

During my time as the Commander of the ISAF. I saw the differences we were making. Later, as Chief of the Defence Staff, I had the privilege of seeing some of our initiatives completed - and many others started.

Canadians should be proud of the work done by their Armed Forces. Because of their hard work and courage Afghanistan is a better place for all Afghans. Open elections have been held for the first time in the country's history, more children are in school, women have greater freedoms, the Afghan police and army have become a professional and trusted part of the Afghanistan government.

Canada paid a great price – including the deaths of 161 of its best citizens – in assisting Afghanistan. Their legacy will live on and I am proud to say I knew them and served with them.

We will remember them.

General (Ret.) Rick Hillier, OC, CMM, ONL, MSC, CD
former Chief of the Defence Staff - Feb 2005 to July 2008

NO QUESTION OF INTENT!

On 11 September 2001, the world was shocked to hear that a passenger aircraft had crashed into one of the World Trade Center towers in New York City. At first, most believed that a terrible accident had occured. Then a second plane hit the twin towers and a third hit the Pentagon in Washington DC. Brave passengers on a fourth hijacked plane forced it to crash in rural Pennsylvania. It was abundantly clear that whatever was happening - was no accident.

Within minutes pictures were being broadcast around the world of two burning towers and a collapsed portion of the Pentagon. The photos were dramatic and telling – people were injured and many would die.

Earlier that day, in a well-planned and coordinated action, 19 men boarded flights intent on delivering a spectacular blow against the West. Five hijackers boarded American Airlines Flight 11 at Boston's Logan Airport joining 76 passengers and a crew of 11 bound for Los Angeles on the 8:00 am flight.

At almost the same time United Airlines Flight 175 left Boston also headed to Los Angeles with nine crew, 51 passengers and five terrorists onboard. In Washington DC, five more hijackers boarded American Airlines Flight 77 at Dulles International Airport. The Los Angeles bound flight had a crew of six and 53 passengers all settling in for the long cross country trip. Finally, at Newark International Airport, United Airlines Flight 93 was preparing to head to San Francisco with seven crew, 33 passengers - and four hijackers.

The planes were large (two Boeing 757s and two 767s) and were fully loaded with fuel. Almost immediately after take-off, the hijackers commandeered the planes using mace, box cutters and hand tools they had smuggled on board.

In previous hijackings, hostages had been used by the terrorists to gain money or political considerations. This was different – very different. This time, the hijackers were not interested in taking hostages - they intended to fly the planes into very public targets causing massive casualties. These were not hijackings – they were suicide missions.

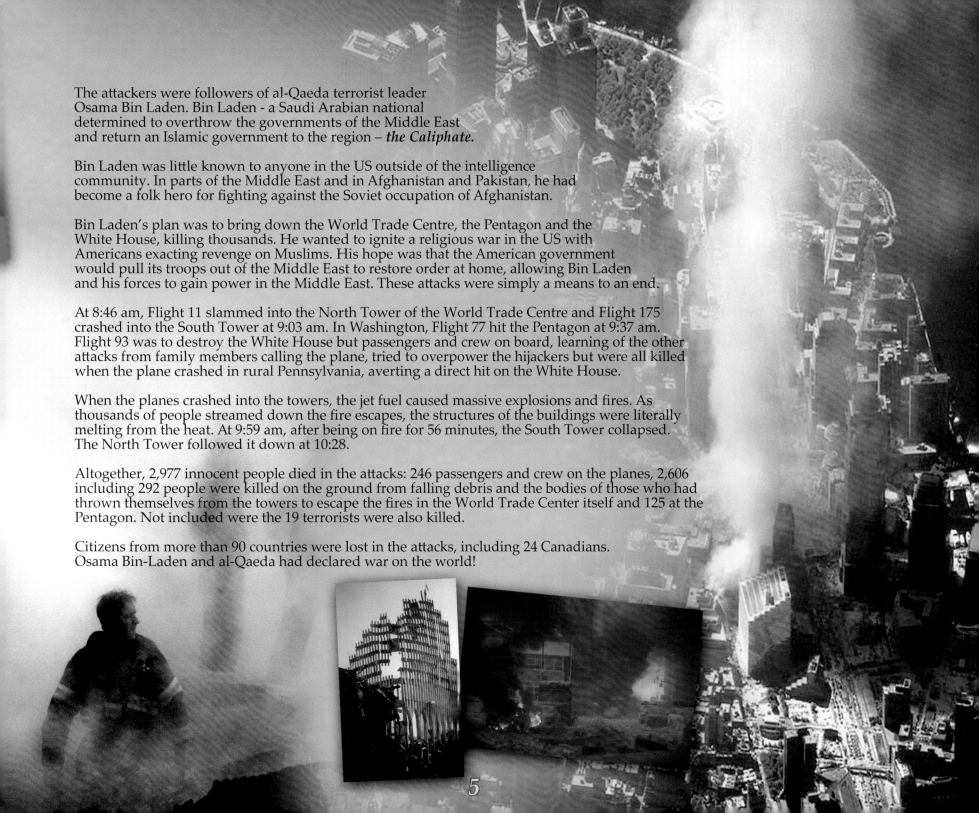

The attackers were followers of al-Qaeda terrorist leader Osama Bin Laden. Bin Laden - a Saudi Arabian national determined to overthrow the governments of the Middle East and return an Islamic government to the region – *the Caliphate.*

Bin Laden was little known to anyone in the US outside of the intelligence community. In parts of the Middle East and in Afghanistan and Pakistan, he had become a folk hero for fighting against the Soviet occupation of Afghanistan.

Bin Laden's plan was to bring down the World Trade Centre, the Pentagon and the White House, killing thousands. He wanted to ignite a religious war in the US with Americans exacting revenge on Muslims. His hope was that the American government would pull its troops out of the Middle East to restore order at home, allowing Bin Laden and his forces to gain power in the Middle East. These attacks were simply a means to an end.

At 8:46 am, Flight 11 slammed into the North Tower of the World Trade Centre and Flight 175 crashed into the South Tower at 9:03 am. In Washington, Flight 77 hit the Pentagon at 9:37 am. Flight 93 was to destroy the White House but passengers and crew on board, learning of the other attacks from family members calling the plane, tried to overpower the hijackers but were all killed when the plane crashed in rural Pennsylvania, averting a direct hit on the White House.

When the planes crashed into the towers, the jet fuel caused massive explosions and fires. As thousands of people streamed down the fire escapes, the structures of the buildings were literally melting from the heat. At 9:59 am, after being on fire for 56 minutes, the South Tower collapsed. The North Tower followed it down at 10:28.

Altogether, 2,977 innocent people died in the attacks: 246 passengers and crew on the planes, 2,606 including 292 people were killed on the ground from falling debris and the bodies of those who had thrown themselves from the towers to escape the fires in the World Trade Center itself and 125 at the Pentagon. Not included were the 19 terrorists were also killed.

Citizens from more than 90 countries were lost in the attacks, including 24 Canadians. Osama Bin-Laden and al-Qaeda had declared war on the world!

CANADA'S ROLE IN PEACEKEEPING

In the trying times following World War Two, the world was left reeling. Fifty million people had been killed, including six million Jews slaughtered by the Nazis in a systematic genocide. Hundreds of millions were homeless and the economies of entire countries were decimated.

In 1945, 51 countries, including Canada, gathered to build an organization, the United Nations (UN), focused on peace in the world and in the hope that a world war would never again happen. During the planning stages, the UN contemplated the idea of having a standing army of its own, using troops and equipment borrowed from the member nations. The force was to be a real and imminent response to those who would threaten world peace.

However, the world was war weary. The major players – the United States, Great Britain, France and even Canada just wanted to put the war behind them. Soldiers, sailors and airmen were being sent home to their farms and shops. Providing troops to the UN seemed an unnecessary hardship and cost. After all, the world had learned its lesson – it knew better than to go to war again.

The UN soon had reason to rethink its decision. First there was Korea in 1950. Then on 26 July 1956, Egypt's newly elected nationalist President Gamal Abdel Nasser, sent armed troops into the Suez Canal zone to seize the waterway from the French who had built it and leased the territory from the Egyptian government. To the French, and the British who used the canal, the Egyptian action was tantamount to a declaration of war and, on 31 October 1956, the two allies started a full out military campaign against the Egyptian armed forces.

The Soviet Union quickly pledged its support to the Egyptian government and the world awoke to the prospect of three superpowers – all nuclear armed – facing off in the deserts of North Africa.

Enter Lester B. Pearson, Canada's Minister of Foreign Affairs. At an emergency meeting of the UN on 7 November 1956 Pearson proposed a United Nations Emergency Force. The force was to be made up of countries not directly involved in the conflict and would be inserted between the combatants, allowing each side to withdraw without "surrendering" to the enemy. Within a week, UN troops were landing in the Suez Canal Zone.

Pearson went on to win the Nobel Peace Prize for his efforts and Canada would, until 2002, participate in every single peacekeeping mission authorized by the United Nations. It is the only country in the world that can make that claim.

For Canadian troops, the classic form of peacekeeping came in Cyprus. The island nation, located in the Mediterranean, was split between the Turks in the north and the Greeks in the south. A series of conflicts and finally a civil war on the island drew the United Nations, and Canada, into a peacekeeping role as early as 1964.

Canadian troops were on the ground patrolling the "Green Line" between the Greeks and the Turks to prevent an all-out war. Both the NATO (the North Atlantic Treaty Organization) and the UN had an interest in keeping the peace as Greece and Turkey were members of both organizations.

Canada would stay in Cyprus for 29 years, providing security and aid to Greek and Turkish Cypriots.

At the same time, Canada sent troops to places as diverse as the Middle East, Africa and Southeast Asia. Canadian peacekeepers seemed to be everywhere.

In 1992, the UN passed a resolution to intercede in the on-going strife in the former Yugoslavia. A civil war had degenerated to genocide and the world could no longer remain neutral. There was no peace to "keep." Neither side wanted UN intervention as they were more focused on gaining territory than they were on human rights.

The 1945 decision to not have a standing force now caused problems. Without military options, the UN turned to NATO and asked its member countries to do "the heavy lifting." Soon NATO troops including Canadians were taking an active role in everything from protecting refugees to negotiating between the belligerents.

Canadian soldiers, at a place called the Medak Pocket, would face their greatest firefight since the Korean War. Troops were fully armed and equipped, not for peacekeeping, but for combat. Lester Pearson would never have recognized what was happening in Croatia, Bosnia, Kosovo and Serbia as peacekeeping, but it was what the world asked of Canada, and Canadians.

Then 9/11 happened...

THE UN AND NATO RESPOND

As the smoke was still curling from the destroyed World Trade Centre Buildings, the hunt for those responsible was beginning.

Afghanistan had been in the state of civil war for years. When the Soviets withdrew from the country after 10 years of occupation, a power vacuum was left in their place. A radical – and fundamentalist – Muslim group known as the Taliban had come to power in the country. Regional warlords fought with both the central government and each other as land and trade routes changed hands regularly.

In the mix was a group virtually unknown to those outside Afghanistan intelligence circles – al-Qaeda. The group was formed from remnants of fighters who had come from other countries to Afghanistan to fight the Soviets and decided to stay. Led by Osama bin Laden, the group planned terror acts designed to restore the Caliphate – the Muslim empire circa 700 AD.

As part of Afghan culture, the Taliban were compelled to offer sanctuary to the al-Qaeda terrorists who set up training camps in the country. It was at these camps that some of the 9/11 terrorists received their first training.

On 12 September 2001, the United Nations (UN) adopted Resolution 1368 which condemned the attacks and stated in part that the UN "regards such acts, like any act of international terrorism, a threat to international peace and security" and expressed "its readiness to take all necessary steps to respond to the terrorist attacks of 11 September 2001, and to combat all forms of terrorism, in accordance with its responsibilities under the Charter of the United Nations."

For the UN, it was the strongest possible language and raised terrorism to the level of Chapter VII (of the UN Charter) under which the Security Council "may authorize the use of force."

On 28 September, 2001 UN Security Council Resolution 1373 was passed and gave states the authorization to "take the necessary steps to prevent the commission of terrorist acts" and to "cooperate, particularly through bilateral and multilateral arrangements and agreements, to prevent and suppress terrorist attacks and take action against perpetrators of such acts."

At the same time, 12 September 2001, NATO was meeting to discuss its possible responses to the attacks in New York, Washington and Pennsylvania. When the NATO treaty was signed on 4 April 1949, it was established (in Article 5 of the treaty) that "The Parties agree that an armed attack against one or more of them in Europe or North America shall be considered an attack against them all and consequently they agree that, if such an armed attack occurs, each of them, in exercise of the right of individual or collective self-defense…will assist the Party or Parties so attacked."

It was Article 5 to which the Americans referred in the September meeting. Lord Robertson, NATO's secretary general – in a public statement – condemned the actions of the terrorists and urged the "international community and the members of the Alliance to unite their forces in fighting the scourge of terrorism."

For the first time since its formation, NATO under Article 5 of the treaty, agreed to take action on 2 October 2001. Secretary General Lord Robertson confirmed that the Americans had proved that "the individuals who carried out the attacks belonged to the world-wide terrorist network of al-Qaeda, headed by Osama bin Laden and protected by the Taliban regime in Afghanistan."

On 4 October, NATO announced that it fully backed a US led invasion of Afghanistan.

When a coalition of forces led by the United States and Great Britain moved into Afghanistan, it was not under a specific UN resolution but rather under Article 51 which states that there exists "the inherent right of individual or collective self-defense if an armed attack occurs - and requires states to report such actions immediately."

World Wide Al-Queda Activity

United Kingdom
Belgium
Germany
France
Spain — Italy — Syria — Afghanistan
Morocco — Iraq — Pakistan
Algeria — Libya — Saudi Arabia
Mauritania — Yemen
Mali — Niger — Kenya — Somalia — Philippines
Uganda
Tanzania — Indonesia

Map Courtesy WikiMedia

CANADA ENTERS THE FRAY

At the same time that NATO committed to invoking Article 5 of the NATO treaty, Canada was ready to pledge its forces to support the invasion of Afghanistan under the code-name Op APOLLO.

However, even before the NATO commitment became official, Canada was moving to provide forces to the impending war in Afghanistan. Canada often had troops training with American forces. On 20 September 2001, Minister of National Defence, the Honorable Art Eggleton passed the word that Canadian Forces personnel on exchange with the Americans or other NATO allies were allowed to participate in Afghanistan operations with their host countries.

When NATO Secretary General George Robertson committed NATO to the Afghanistan mission, Canada was quick to respond. On 7 October, Canadian Prime Minister, the Right Honorable Jean Chrétien announced to the nation, and the world, that Canada would be committing – air, land and sea resources in support of the U.S. invasion of Afghanistan code-named Op ENDURING FREEDOM. At the Department of National Defense (DND) Headquarters, General Ray Henault, the Chief of the Defence Staff (CDS), was issuing warning orders to Canadian units to prepare for possible combat.

The next day, the Defence Minister confirmed that over 2,000 Canadian Forces (CF) members would be involved in Op APOLLO and that the navy would be the first in.

HMCS Halifax, a Canadian frigate, was in the Persian Gulf and was deployed to assist with Op ENDURING FREEDOM. Canada's Navy would play a major role in both protecting coalition forces and in interdicting shipping involved in smuggling narcotics, arms and people. As Op APOLLO continued, more and more Canadian ships would become involved including the replenishment ships HMCS Preserver and HMCS Protecteur that worked in the Persian Gulf and the Red Sea, replenishing not only Canadian ships but those of other coalition members as well.

While Canada's senior service did not directly engage the enemy, it was involved in a number of significant incidents including when HMCS Algonquin, along with a French warship and Canadian aircraft, boarded a ship carrying al-Qaeda members trying to slip through the coalition net.

The personnel and assets from the Canadian Navy and Air Force who deployed to support Op APOLLO were extremely active and effective.

On 16 November 2001, the Strategic Airlift Detachment from 8 Wing Trenton was galvanized into action. Initially stationed in Germany, the CC-150 Polaris (Airbus A310) and 40 CF members were quickly engaged in the processes of "medical evacuation, sustainment and re-supply, rapid delivery of operationally required items, and movement of personnel into theatre."

With the CC-150 Polaris engaged in the ever increasing tempo of troop and equipment movements, on 27 December 2001, two CP-140 Aurora long-range surveillance and maritime patrol aircraft joined the CF in the Gulf. The new arrivals were soon assisting with wide-area surveillance not possible from ships.

Midway through Op APOLLO (January 2002), three CC-130 Hercules aircraft and over 200 crew and maintenance personnel joined the Canadian Forces tasked with transporting everything from personnel to cargo. Finally, shipborne CH-124 Sea King helicopters rounded out the Canadian air component.

Canada's largest commitment would ultimately come on the ground. In mid-November 2001, the US asked coalition partners to provide ground forces to assist with the provision of humanitarian aid and security to the areas commanded by the Northern Coalition (a loose alliance of local Afghan forces.)

In response, Canada committed 1,000 members of the Immediate Reaction Force (Land) (IRF(L)), drawn mostly from the 3rd Battalion Princess Patricia's Canadian Light Infantry (3 PPCLI) - on 48 hours' notice to deploy.

As could be expected, the situation in Afghanistan was changing daily. By January 2002, Canada had agreed to send the 3 PPCLI Battle Group (BG) to the Kandahar province Afghanistan to be part of a US Army task force, composed primarily of the US 187th Brigade Combat Team out of Fort Campbell, Kentucky.

The 3 PPCLI BG, commanded by LCol Pat Stogran, were supported by a reconnaissance squadron from Lord Strathcona's Horse (Royal Canadians) (LdSH(RC)), a combat engineer squadron from 1 Combat Engineer Regiment (1 CER), personnel from 1 Service Battalion plus other units within Land Force Western Area (LFWA).

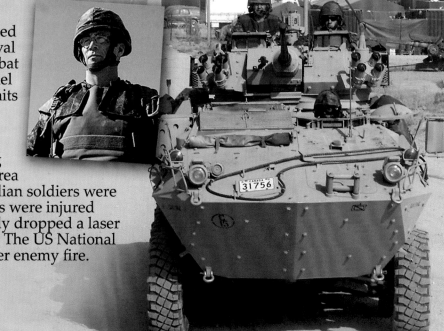

While engaged in a night live firing exercise at Tarnak Farm, training area just outside Kandahar, four Canadian soldiers were accidentally killed and eight others were injured when an American F-16 mistakenly dropped a laser guided 230kg (500-pound) bomb. The US National Guard pilot thought he was under enemy fire.

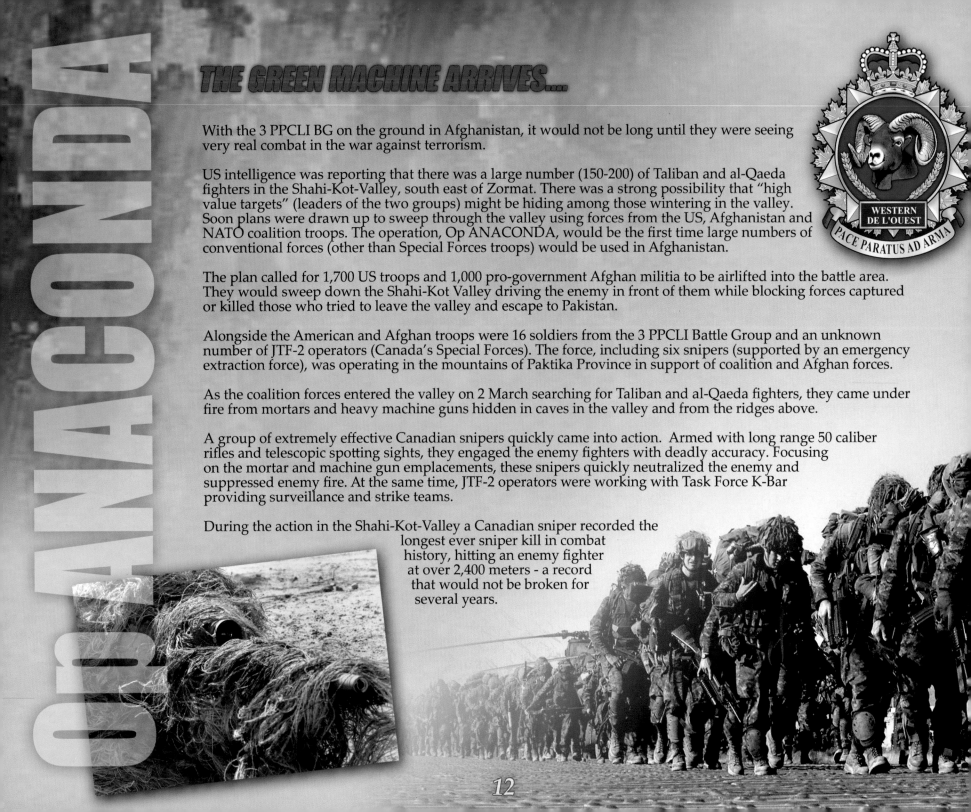

THE GREEN MACHINE ARRIVES....

With the 3 PPCLI BG on the ground in Afghanistan, it would not be long until they were seeing very real combat in the war against terrorism.

US intelligence was reporting that there was a large number (150-200) of Taliban and al-Qaeda fighters in the Shahi-Kot-Valley, south east of Zormat. There was a strong possibility that "high value targets" (leaders of the two groups) might be hiding among those wintering in the valley. Soon plans were drawn up to sweep through the valley using forces from the US, Afghanistan and NATO coalition troops. The operation, Op ANACONDA, would be the first time large numbers of conventional forces (other than Special Forces troops) would be used in Afghanistan.

The plan called for 1,700 US troops and 1,000 pro-government Afghan militia to be airlifted into the battle area. They would sweep down the Shahi-Kot Valley driving the enemy in front of them while blocking forces captured or killed those who tried to leave the valley and escape to Pakistan.

Alongside the American and Afghan troops were 16 soldiers from the 3 PPCLI Battle Group and an unknown number of JTF-2 operators (Canada's Special Forces). The force, including six snipers (supported by an emergency extraction force), was operating in the mountains of Paktika Province in support of coalition and Afghan forces.

As the coalition forces entered the valley on 2 March searching for Taliban and al-Qaeda fighters, they came under fire from mortars and heavy machine guns hidden in caves in the valley and from the ridges above.

A group of extremely effective Canadian snipers quickly came into action. Armed with long range 50 caliber rifles and telescopic spotting sights, they engaged the enemy fighters with deadly accuracy. Focusing on the mortar and machine gun emplacements, these snipers quickly neutralized the enemy and suppressed enemy fire. At the same time, JTF-2 operators were working with Task Force K-Bar providing surveillance and strike teams.

During the action in the Shahi-Kot-Valley a Canadian sniper recorded the longest ever sniper kill in combat history, hitting an enemy fighter at over 2,400 meters - a record that would not be broken for several years.

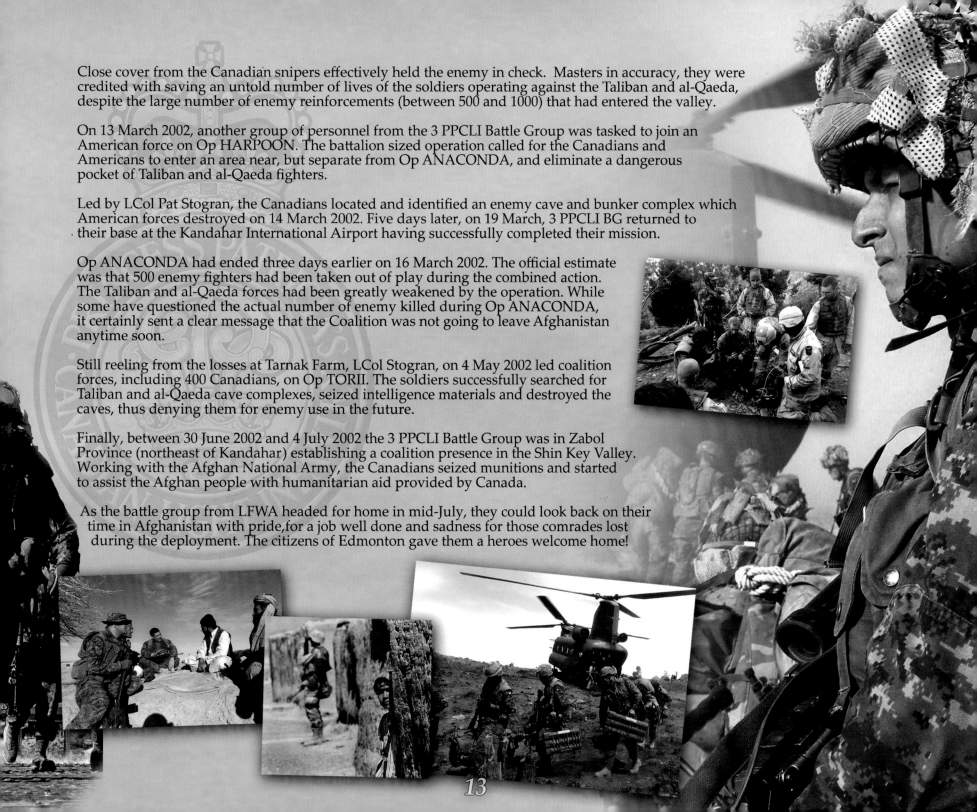

Close cover from the Canadian snipers effectively held the enemy in check. Masters in accuracy, they were credited with saving an untold number of lives of the soldiers operating against the Taliban and al-Qaeda, despite the large number of enemy reinforcements (between 500 and 1000) that had entered the valley.

On 13 March 2002, another group of personnel from the 3 PPCLI Battle Group was tasked to join an American force on Op HARPOON. The battalion sized operation called for the Canadians and Americans to enter an area near, but separate from Op ANACONDA, and eliminate a dangerous pocket of Taliban and al-Qaeda fighters.

Led by LCol Pat Stogran, the Canadians located and identified an enemy cave and bunker complex which American forces destroyed on 14 March 2002. Five days later, on 19 March, 3 PPCLI BG returned to their base at the Kandahar International Airport having successfully completed their mission.

Op ANACONDA had ended three days earlier on 16 March 2002. The official estimate was that 500 enemy fighters had been taken out of play during the combined action. The Taliban and al-Qaeda forces had been greatly weakened by the operation. While some have questioned the actual number of enemy killed during Op ANACONDA, it certainly sent a clear message that the Coalition was not going to leave Afghanistan anytime soon.

Still reeling from the losses at Tarnak Farm, LCol Stogran, on 4 May 2002 led coalition forces, including 400 Canadians, on Op TORII. The soldiers successfully searched for Taliban and al-Qaeda cave complexes, seized intelligence materials and destroyed the caves, thus denying them for enemy use in the future.

Finally, between 30 June 2002 and 4 July 2002 the 3 PPCLI Battle Group was in Zabol Province (northeast of Kandahar) establishing a coalition presence in the Shin Key Valley. Working with the Afghan National Army, the Canadians seized munitions and started to assist the Afghan people with humanitarian aid provided by Canada.

As the battle group from LFWA headed for home in mid-July, they could look back on their time in Afghanistan with pride, for a job well done and sadness for those comrades lost during the deployment. The citizens of Edmonton gave them a heroes welcome home!

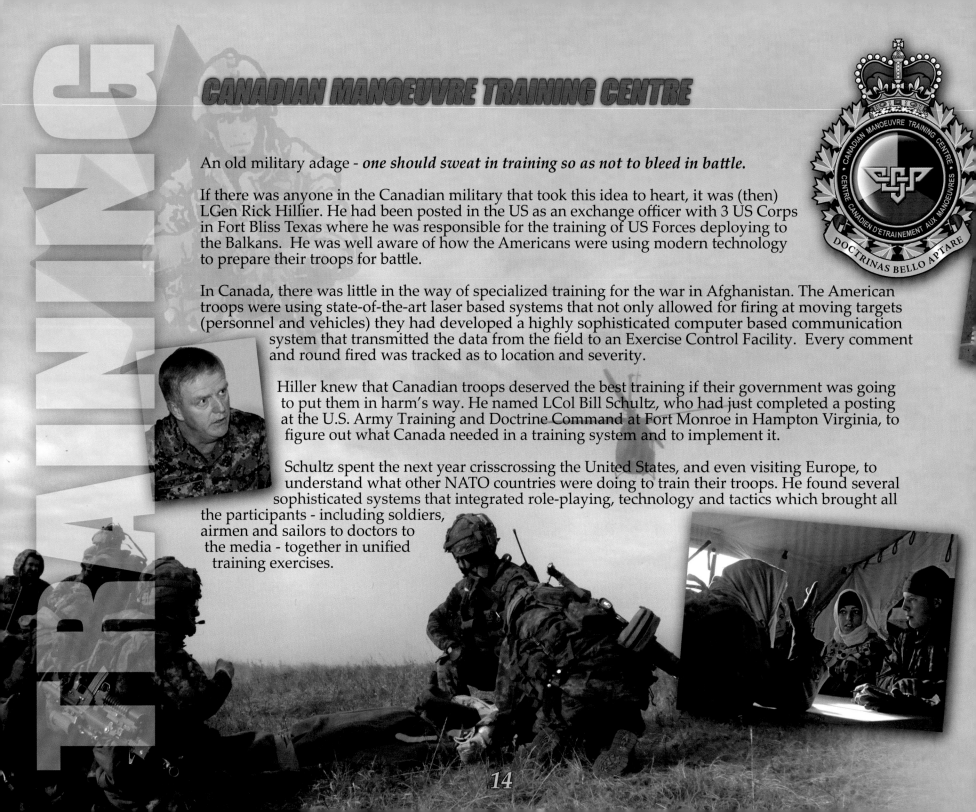

CANADIAN MANOEUVRE TRAINING CENTRE

An old military adage - *one should sweat in training so as not to bleed in battle.*

If there was anyone in the Canadian military that took this idea to heart, it was (then) LGen Rick Hillier. He had been posted in the US as an exchange officer with 3 US Corps in Fort Bliss Texas where he was responsible for the training of US Forces deploying to the Balkans. He was well aware of how the Americans were using modern technology to prepare their troops for battle.

In Canada, there was little in the way of specialized training for the war in Afghanistan. The American troops were using state-of-the-art laser based systems that not only allowed for firing at moving targets (personnel and vehicles) they had developed a highly sophisticated computer based communication system that transmitted the data from the field to an Exercise Control Facility. Every comment and round fired was tracked as to location and severity.

Hiller knew that Canadian troops deserved the best training if their government was going to put them in harm's way. He named LCol Bill Schultz, who had just completed a posting at the U.S. Army Training and Doctrine Command at Fort Monroe in Hampton Virginia, to figure out what Canada needed in a training system and to implement it.

Schultz spent the next year crisscrossing the United States, and even visiting Europe, to understand what other NATO countries were doing to train their troops. He found several sophisticated systems that integrated role-playing, technology and tactics which brought all the participants - including soldiers, airmen and sailors to doctors to the media - together in unified training exercises.

It was a given that Canada needed to train its people at least as well as its allies did. Camp Wainwright, located 210 km east of Edmonton Alberta, was chosen as the site for the new Canadian Manoeuvre Training Centre (CMTC). Camp Wainwright was well known to Canadian soldiers as a sparse but realistic training ground. The challenge was to create a new infrastructure to support LGen Hiller's vision.

In 2003 the DND chose the Weapons Effects Simulation (WES) as the system that would provide the real-life training necessary and testing began. With the WES system, each soldier wears an assortment of laser detectors that record hits from everything from a rifle to chemical agents.

In real time, each and every hit is recorded and analysed giving the soldier – and those monitoring the system - real time information on the severity of the hit and its impact on the battlefield. If a soldier was wounded, he would have to wait for medics to arrive who, provided with the information from the system, were able to deliver the appropriate treatment before transporting the victim. If the soldier "died", he had to spend six hours out of action.

The WES system not only worked on soldiers but on vehicles as well. If a vehicle is struck with a round or IED, the amount of "damage" can be quickly and accurately assessed.

All of the data, supported by video camera feeds, was collected in the Exercise Control (EXCON) centre and enabled the umpires and staff to playback and review exercises involving as many as 2000 troops and 700 vehicles.

Pre-deployment training for Afghanistan did not end with technology. If the Canadians being deployed were to really understand what they were facing in the war in places like Kabul and Kandahar, they would need to experience it.

To make the training as realistic as possible, the Canadian military built six large and 10 small Afghan villages at Camp Wainwright. Each village came with its own villagers (actors trained for the part) including religious leaders, civilians such as farmer and shopkeepers and, of course, the media. The villagers wore the same laser vests as the soldiers – if a villager was shot, the aftermath would have to be dealt with.

The goal of the CMTC, WES and Wainwright was to make it safer for Canadian soldiers to operate in Afghanistan. By early 2007, it was clearly proving its worth.

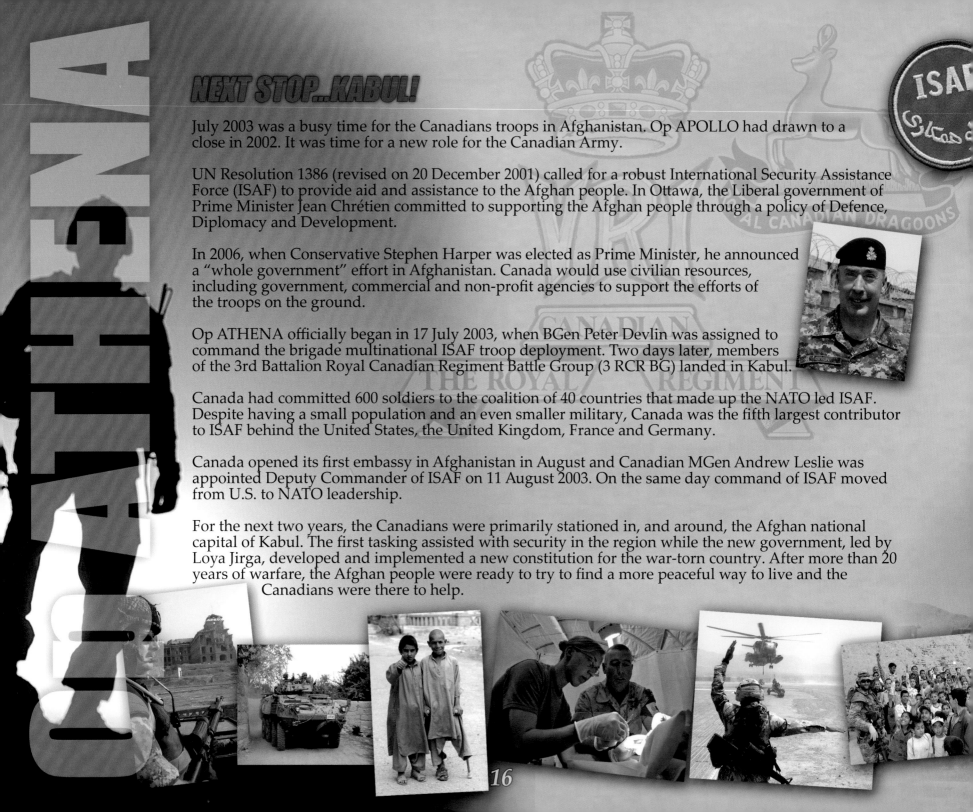

NEXT STOP...KABUL!

July 2003 was a busy time for the Canadians troops in Afghanistan. Op APOLLO had drawn to a close in 2002. It was time for a new role for the Canadian Army.

UN Resolution 1386 (revised on 20 December 2001) called for a robust International Security Assistance Force (ISAF) to provide aid and assistance to the Afghan people. In Ottawa, the Liberal government of Prime Minister Jean Chrétien committed to supporting the Afghan people through a policy of Defence, Diplomacy and Development.

In 2006, when Conservative Stephen Harper was elected as Prime Minister, he announced a "whole government" effort in Afghanistan. Canada would use civilian resources, including government, commercial and non-profit agencies to support the efforts of the troops on the ground.

Op ATHENA officially began in 17 July 2003, when BGen Peter Devlin was assigned to command the brigade multinational ISAF troop deployment. Two days later, members of the 3rd Battalion Royal Canadian Regiment Battle Group (3 RCR BG) landed in Kabul.

Canada had committed 600 soldiers to the coalition of 40 countries that made up the NATO led ISAF. Despite having a small population and an even smaller military, Canada was the fifth largest contributor to ISAF behind the United States, the United Kingdom, France and Germany.

Canada opened its first embassy in Afghanistan in August and Canadian MGen Andrew Leslie was appointed Deputy Commander of ISAF on 11 August 2003. On the same day command of ISAF moved from U.S. to NATO leadership.

For the next two years, the Canadians were primarily stationed in, and around, the Afghan national capital of Kabul. The first tasking assisted with security in the region while the new government, led by Loya Jirga, developed and implemented a new constitution for the war-torn country. After more than 20 years of warfare, the Afghan people were ready to try to find a more peaceful way to live and the Canadians were there to help.

Perhaps the most important task completed by the Canadians, who now made up 40% of ISAF, in the Kabul phase of Op ATHENA, occurred after Canadian Lieutenant-General Rick Hillier took command of ISAF on 9 February 2004. The Afghan government had announced that, for the first time ever, Afghans would be allowed to democratically elect their own government in elections on 9 October 2004. Hillier, the Canadians and ISAF were given the responsibility of ensuring the safety and security of the process. It would prove to be a real challenge as the Taliban pushed back with violence.

In 2005, with the Kabul region relatively secure, ISAF turned to the most violent area of the country – Kandahar Province. The plan was to "ramp up" a Provincial Reconstruction Team (PRT) in the region to help the Afghans build schools, hospitals, effective police forces and a functional justice system. The coalition asked Canada to move to the region and take over. The Canadian government agreed to commit 500 additional troops, plus medical and dental teams as well as diplomats, engineers, police and correctional officers.

From May to November 2006, Canada commanded the Multinational Brigade Command (South). During this time, Canadian troops of the 1 RCR BG engaged the Taliban during Op MEDUSA as part of the Second Battle of Panjwaii. Op MEDUSA was the deadliest battle for Canada since the Korean War - with 12 Canadian fatalities.

By the time Canada's Op ATHENA came to an end in December 2011, over 40,000 Canadians had served in Afghanistan. This was the largest deployment of Canadians since WWII and ultimately saw TF Kandahar grow to brigade size including an Air Wing known as Task Force Silver Dart.

American forces took over from the Canadians on 15 December 2011, BGen Chuck Lamarre was the last Canadian soldier to leave Kandahar - seen here presenting the camp flag to LGen Stuart Beare, Commander of Canadian Expeditionary Force Command (CEFCOM).

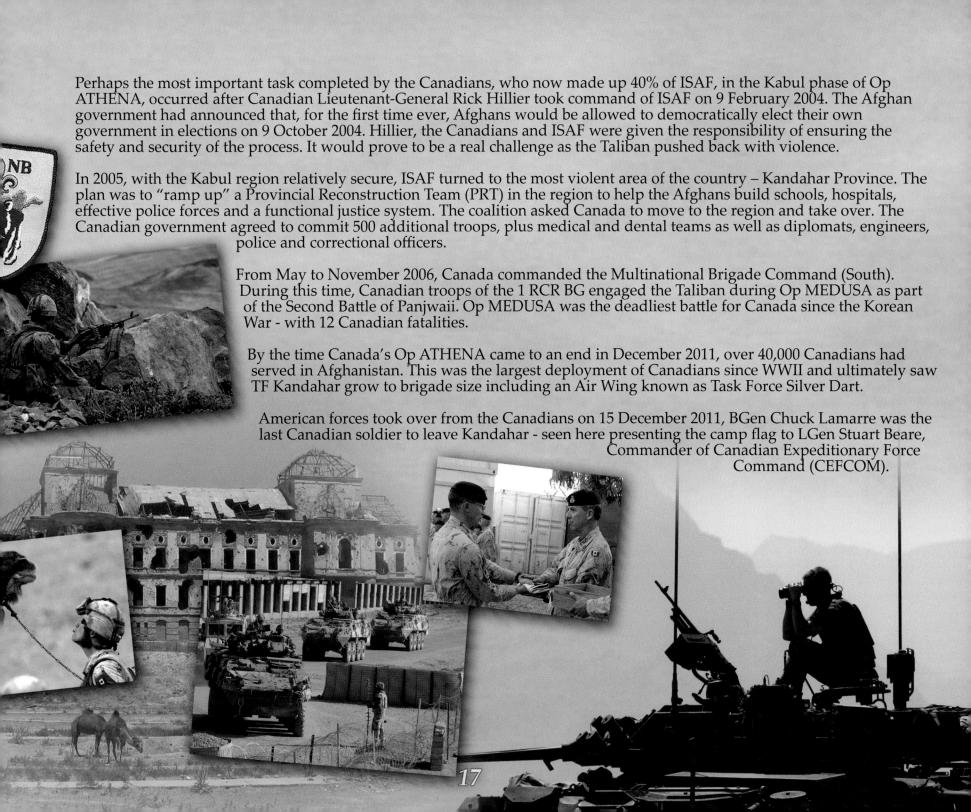

CANADIAN CAMPS..."OVER THERE"

For Canadians at home, Afghanistan was somewhere on the other side of the world. They might have had a vague idea where the country was on a map, but to understand the complex geography and culture was a bit more of a challenge.

For most, names like Camp Julien, Camp Nathan Smith and the Kandahar Air Field (KAF) all rolled into one. However, to the men and women serving in Afghanistan, the camps took on the roles of workplace, shelter, safe haven and for a while – home.

Camp Julien, in Kabul, was ready and waiting for the 3 RCR BG when they arrived in August of 2003. It was part of Canada's future – and its past - named for Lance Corporal George Patrick Julien, a member of the RCR's who distinguished himself in Korea on Hill 187 in May 1953 when he won the Military Medal.

From Camp Julien in Kabul, over 2,000 Canadian soldiers fought for the security of Afghanistan in the early days of the conflict. They were supported by over 400 civilian workers – most from Nepal. The civilians provided everything from administrative to laundry and food services.

Canada continued to operate Camp Julien until Nov 2005 when the Canadian Forces moved to Kandahar province in the southern region of Afghanistan.

The camp was converted in 2007 to the Counter Insurgency (COIN) Academy where military leaders from Afghanistan could take courses in counter insurgency operations.

KAF was the new home for the Canadian Contingent in Afghanistan starting in November of 2005. Originally built by the Americans in the 1960s as the Kandahar International Airport, it is the second largest airport in Afghanistan.

During the 1980s, the Soviets captured and occupied the airport, followed by the warlord Gul Agha Sherzai in 1992 and then the Taliban in 1994. Op ENDURING FREEDOM, in 2001 returned the airport to coalition forces – and Afghan control.

Located 16 kilometres south-east of Kandahar City, KAF was converted to a fully operating military base and supported over 200 military aircraft, as well as military forces from around the world including the Afghan Armed Forces (AFF) and the Afghanistan National Police (ANP).

In March 2006, Canadian BGen David Fraser took command of the multi-national brigade, which included the 1 PPCLI BG, both headquartered at KAF. The Canadians at KAF totaled 2,250 and were tasked with improving the security situation in southern Afghanistan.

KAF was like a small city – fully equipped to make the lives of the Canadian soldiers as comfortable as possible (though no one had any illusions their situation was "army-comfortable.")

As time went on, more and more facilities were developed including: a full recreation centre with billiards, air hockey and ping pong tables, a movie theater, a library, retail stores and restaurants, multiple sports fields and a chapel. To make the Canadians feel even more at home, a fully operational Tim Horton's coffee shop, a Canadian icon, was positioned at a place called 'The Boardwalk'.

When the Canadians left KAF for the last time, in March 2011, there were over 26,000 people living and working on the base.

At the same time Canadians were living on - and fighting from - the Kandahar Airfield, the Kandahar Provincial Reconstruction Team (KPRT) was operating from Camp Nathan Smith in the heart of Kandahar City.

A former fruit canning factory, the Camp was first occupied by American soldiers from Fort Bragg North Carolina before being turned over to the Canadians in 2005. It was named for Private Nathan Smith, a 3PPCLI casualty of the Tarnak farm incident.

Equipped with a local bazaar, an aid station, a gym, a fire fighting reservoir (swimming pool) and two dining facilities, Camp Nathan Smith was often the site of meetings with local and national Afghan leaders.

In July 2010, Canada vacated Camp Nathan Smith. Today the camp is an ANP post.

INTO THE VALLEY RODE THE 11,000!

This time the outcome would be a much different than what was experienced by the ill-fated Light Brigade!

For the 2,200 Canadian troops preparing for battle in June 2006, Op MOUNTAIN THRUST was to be the largest coalition operation in Afghanistan since 2001. The Canadians were joined by more than 2,300 troops from the United States, 3,300 from Great Britain and 3,500 Afghan soldiers plus soldiers from Australia, Romania and the Czech Republic. In all, 11,000 troops would engage the Taliban, which had recently ramped up the violence in southern Afghanistan. The goal was to drive the insurgents out - in advance of NATO officially taking control of the area.

US Major-General S.P. Freakly, Commander of all operations in Afghanistan, explained to the media that the troops would concentrate their efforts in western Uruzgan and north-eastern Helmand provinces while pockets of insurgents around Kandahar and in Zabul province would also receive attention. The official goal was to "take out the security threat and establish conditions where government forces, government institutions [and] humanitarian organizations could move in and begin the real work."

At the sharp end was the 1 PPCLI Battle Group. Their orders were to move through the Zari and Panjwaii regions south of Highway 1 and neutralize or capture any of the enemy they encountered.

The Canadians expected to face stiff resistance. The region was heavily frequented by the Taliban, who used the small villages as both hideouts and sources of supplies, food and protection. Highway 1 was a major transportation route for the insurgents. While the ANP did set up checkpoints along the highway, the Taliban seemed to move with impunity.

The Coalition Task Force (CTF) was under the command of Canadian BGen David Fraser. For their part in Op MOUNTAIN THRUST, 1 PPCLI was to work in concert with both the ANP and ANA.

B Coy, 1PPCLI, was first into the fray, establishing Patrol Base Wilson, a Forward Operating Base (FOB) named for MCpl Tim Wilson of Grande Prairie, AB, killed earlier in the year. The goal was to establish a permanent Canadian presence in the Zari region, observe, monitor and suppress enemy activity in the area.

C Coy, 1 PPCLI, along with its contingent of Afghan National Army (ANA) troops, headed west into Registan – the desert region of Helmand and Kandahar. C Coy would concentrate on clearing each small village in the area – one house at a time. The Canadians made their first contact with the enemy and two soldiers were injured by enemy small arms fire.

The fighting raged throughout June and July 2006. Ultimately, over 1,100 Taliban paid the price with their lives while another 400 were captured. Most of the deaths came as the result of heavy coalition aerial bombing raids.

Despite the heavy death-toll among the enemy, Op MOUNTAIN THRUST did little to stop the violence against Afghan citizens and coalition forces. In fact, at one point in late July, the Taliban rallied long enough to capture two districts of Helmand Province – two districts the coalition had to retake from the enemy.

In the end, 150 coalition soldiers died and 40 Afghan policemen were taken hostage. Ultimately, the Taliban remained a very real threat in Southern Afghanistan as NATO took command of the area.

TALIBAN FACES THE MIGHT OF ORION

On 17 May 2006, Canada lost another soldier to the enemy but this time is was different. There had been a number of running battles with the Taliban that day and, in one of them, Captain Nic (Nichola) Goddard, a very capable and respected artillery officer, became the first female combat arms officer killed in Canadian history.

Later that day, in another hostile contact with the enemy, Canadian Sergeant Michael Denine of 8 Platoon, Charlie Coy, 1 PPCLI earned the Medal of Military Valour – the third highest honour the country can bestow for bravery.

The month of May had been particularly difficult for the Canadians. There had been an increase in violence in the Panjwaii region following an uneasy calm that had lasted for a number of months.

As the 1 PPCLI Battle Group took to the field, it was as Task Force Orion commanded by LCol Ian C. Hope. From 23 May to 14 June 2006, TF Orion engaged in 37 separate firefights with Taliban groups of 30-40 fighters each in the Panjwaii and Zharii districts.

By mid-July 2006, TF Orion was joined by Canadian and Afghan troops participating in Op MOUNTAIN THRUST. From 8 through 12 July, the Canadians and their allies faced extremely heavy fighting - but Taliban groups in Pashmul and Panjwaii were soon in retreat, moving toward refuge in Pakistan.

With no chance to rest, TF Orion quickly turned to assisting the British troops fighting in OP HEWAD – an operation focused on clearing the Taliban from Sangin in Helmand Province. On 13 July, the Canadians were fighting to rescue a group of British soldiers besieged in the centre of Sangin.

After assisting the British, TF Orion was again engaged in multiple firefights, effectively neutralizing the enemy, but with no Canadian losses. On 17 July, supported by three US Special Forces teams, TF Orion was ordered to retake the Taliban-controlled towns of Nawa and Garmsir – a task completed in 24 hours. The Canadians remained in Helmand, working along side the British for another week.

Canadians proved they were a force to be reckoned with!

PANJWAII

OPERATION ARCHER

20 06

TASK FORCE ORION

The return to Panjwaii was not a peaceful one for the Canadians. Resuming operations on 2 August, just 24 hours later, four soldiers were killed and 11 injured in Pashmul while the Task Force killed or wounded 90 Taliban fighters, including three commanders. This was in the midst of 1 RCR BG taking over for much of Op MEDUSA.

TF Orion's actions in Pashmul had derailed a Taliban plan to attack Kandahar City itself. Weakened, the Taliban chose to attack Panjwaii District Centre on 19 August (Afghan Independence Day), hoping that it would not be as well defended as Kandahar. If fact, A Coy, 2 PPCLI put up a stiff (and successful) resistance, killing or wounding over 70 of the enemy.

In September, Op MEDUSA again took the fight to the Taliban. The costs were very heavy, with 12 Canadian soldiers killed in Canada's greatest combat losses since Korea.

Throughout the Battle of Panjwaii, the Canadians had been careful to not fire on civilians despite the Taliban having no reluctance to hide among the civilian population including in private homes.

The Taliban hoped that by using this tactic, the Canadians and other coalition members would not call in bombings and air strikes. Their plan did not work! To avoid civilian casualties, the coalition quickly changed their air tactics - and waged a very successful and devastating campaign against the Taliban.

While the Battle of Panjwaii ended in October 2006, the terrorist attacks did not. The Canadians faced a regular barrage of mortars, bombs and small arms fire. In November, CWO R.M.J. Girouard, the RSM of 1RCR, Cpl A.H. Storm and an American soldier were killed by IEDs.

To support the troops on the ground, the Canadian government agreed to a military request for a squadron of Leopard C2 tanks to be moved to Kandahar. On 2 December, the tanks rolled in from KAF to the Panjwaii FOB where they quickly got the attention of the Taliban fighters in the region who attacked them, ineffectively, with small arms and rocket propelled grenades.

As the Leopards fired back at the Taliban, it was the first time Canadians had used tanks in combat since the NATO action in Kosovo.

AFGHANISTAN

KANDAHAR

mand
vince

< PANJWAII

Kandahar
Province

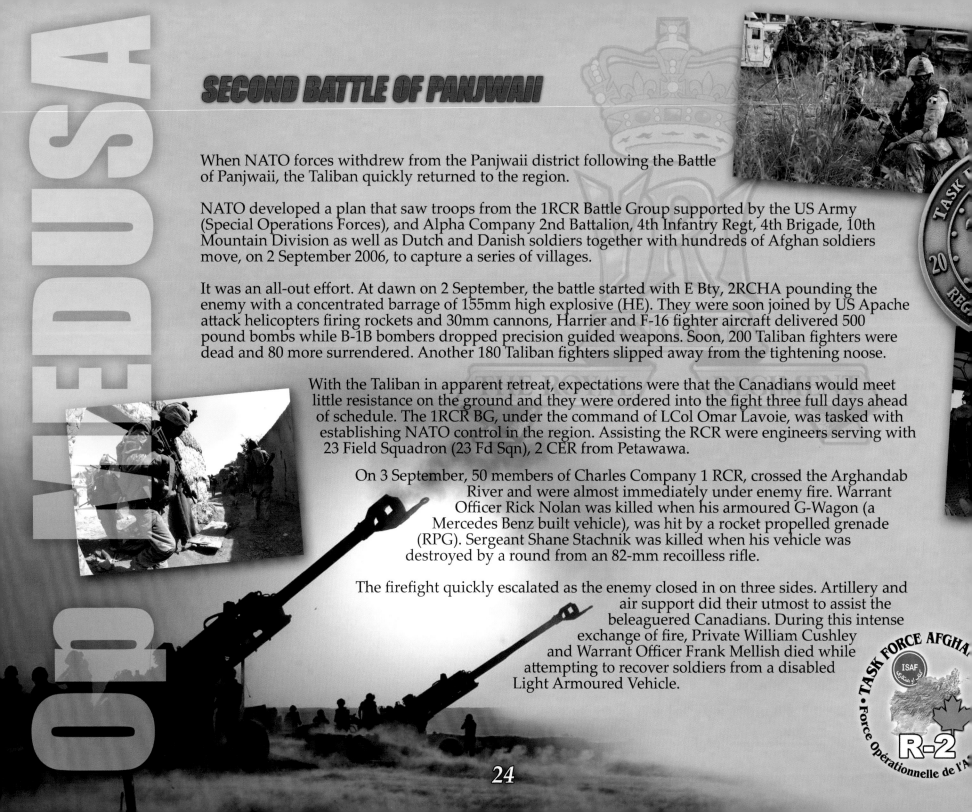

SECOND BATTLE OF PANJWAII

When NATO forces withdrew from the Panjwaii district following the Battle of Panjwaii, the Taliban quickly returned to the region.

NATO developed a plan that saw troops from the 1RCR Battle Group supported by the US Army (Special Operations Forces), and Alpha Company 2nd Battalion, 4th Infantry Regt, 4th Brigade, 10th Mountain Division as well as Dutch and Danish soldiers together with hundreds of Afghan soldiers move, on 2 September 2006, to capture a series of villages.

It was an all-out effort. At dawn on 2 September, the battle started with E Bty, 2RCHA pounding the enemy with a concentrated barrage of 155mm high explosive (HE). They were soon joined by US Apache attack helicopters firing rockets and 30mm cannons, Harrier and F-16 fighter aircraft delivered 500 pound bombs while B-1B bombers dropped precision guided weapons. Soon, 200 Taliban fighters were dead and 80 more surrendered. Another 180 Taliban fighters slipped away from the tightening noose.

With the Taliban in apparent retreat, expectations were that the Canadians would meet little resistance on the ground and they were ordered into the fight three full days ahead of schedule. The 1RCR BG, under the command of LCol Omar Lavoie, was tasked with establishing NATO control in the region. Assisting the RCR were engineers serving with 23 Field Squadron (23 Fd Sqn), 2 CER from Petawawa.

On 3 September, 50 members of Charles Company 1 RCR, crossed the Arghandab River and were almost immediately under enemy fire. Warrant Officer Rick Nolan was killed when his armoured G-Wagon (a Mercedes Benz built vehicle), was hit by a rocket propelled grenade (RPG). Sergeant Shane Stachnik was killed when his vehicle was destroyed by a round from an 82-mm recoilless rifle.

The firefight quickly escalated as the enemy closed in on three sides. Artillery and air support did their utmost to assist the beleaguered Canadians. During this intense exchange of fire, Private William Cushley and Warrant Officer Frank Mellish died while attempting to recover soldiers from a disabled Light Armoured Vehicle.

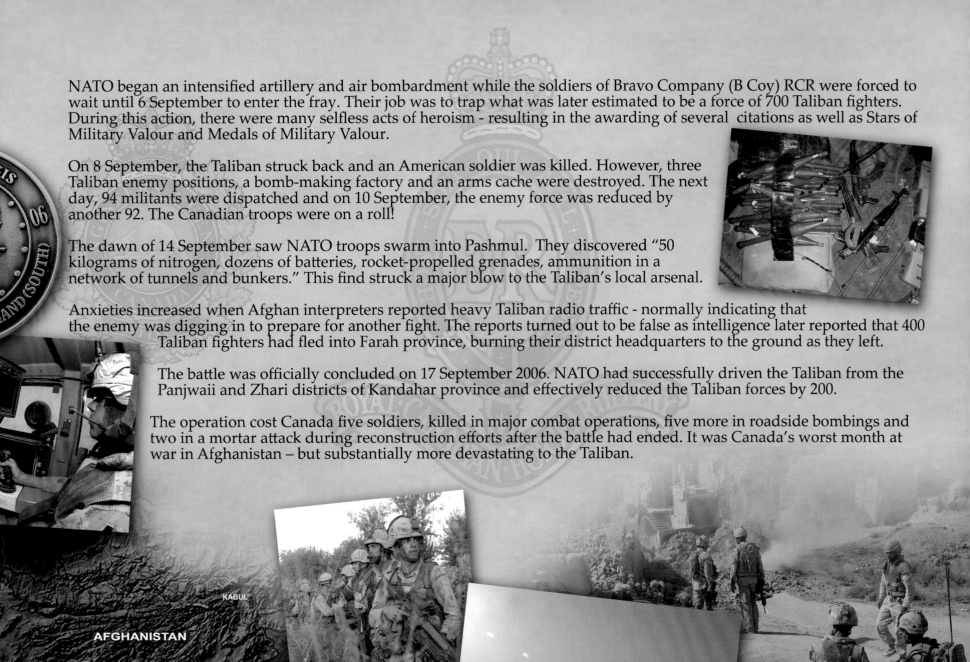

NATO began an intensified artillery and air bombardment while the soldiers of Bravo Company (B Coy) RCR were forced to wait until 6 September to enter the fray. Their job was to trap what was later estimated to be a force of 700 Taliban fighters. During this action, there were many selfless acts of heroism - resulting in the awarding of several citations as well as Stars of Military Valour and Medals of Military Valour.

On 8 September, the Taliban struck back and an American soldier was killed. However, three Taliban enemy positions, a bomb-making factory and an arms cache were destroyed. The next day, 94 militants were dispatched and on 10 September, the enemy force was reduced by another 92. The Canadian troops were on a roll!

The dawn of 14 September saw NATO troops swarm into Pashmul. They discovered "50 kilograms of nitrogen, dozens of batteries, rocket-propelled grenades, ammunition in a network of tunnels and bunkers." This find struck a major blow to the Taliban's local arsenal.

Anxieties increased when Afghan interpreters reported heavy Taliban radio traffic - normally indicating that the enemy was digging in to prepare for another fight. The reports turned out to be false as intelligence later reported that 400 Taliban fighters had fled into Farah province, burning their district headquarters to the ground as they left.

The battle was officially concluded on 17 September 2006. NATO had successfully driven the Taliban from the Panjwaii and Zhari districts of Kandahar province and effectively reduced the Taliban forces by 200.

The operation cost Canada five soldiers, killed in major combat operations, five more in roadside bombings and two in a mortar attack during reconstruction efforts after the battle had ended. It was Canada's worst month at war in Afghanistan – but substantially more devastating to the Taliban.

KABUL

AFGHANISTAN

KANDAHAR

PANJWAII

Kandahar Province

25

PROVINCIAL RECONSTRUCTION TEAMS

For many, the conflict in Afghanistan was about defeating the Taliban and al-Qaeda. The media often covered the stories of the battles and fatalities of Canadian and other coalition soldiers fighting in the country.

It was clear that the Taliban were not about to leave Afghanistan in peace - and that the war was necessary if Afghanistan was ever to be a modern country. However, it was just as clear that force alone would not bring prosperity and peace.

When the CF moved to the region, the Kandahar Provincial Reconstruction Team (KPRT) was quickly established. Headquartered at Camp Nathan Smith, it was made up of 350 diplomats, development experts, corrections experts, police officers (both RCMP and local Canadian police) and a the majority of military personnel (combining engineers, military police, project managers, planners and force protection elements.)

Civil-Military Cooperation (CIMIC) Teams played an important role in the KPRT as they provided the expertise of reservists who understood the military culture, as well as complimentary civilian skill sets in negotiation, project-planning, construction and management expertise.

The KPRTs were designed to "help the democratically elected government of Afghanistan increase its ability to govern, rebuild the nation and provide services to its citizens." When the CF arrived in 2005, Kandahar was one of the most problematic regions in Afghanistan - few families had even the basic necessities of life.

Canada focused on using the PRT to support the "Afghanistan Compact" (a five-year NATO agenda to consolidate democratic institutions, curb insecurity, control the illegal drug trade, stimulate the economy, enforce the law, provide basic services to the Afghan people and protect human rights). The KPRT also gave aid to the Afghan National Development Strategy (the Government of Afghanistan's strategies for security, governance, economic growth and poverty reduction) and the National Solidarity Program (the rehabilitation and development of approximately 5000 villages in Afghanistan.)

The KPRT worked to ensure that four major goals were addressed in the Kandahar region:

1) **Create and maintain a secure environment and establish law and order;**
2) **Provide jobs, education, and essential services (water etc);**
3) **Provide humanitarian assistance to people in need, including refugees; and**
4) **Enhance the management and security of the Afghanistan-Pakistan border.**

Nationally, Canada committed to helping Afghanistan as a whole by building Afghan institutions that were central to the Kandahar priorities and support democratic processes such as elections and contributing to Afghan-led political reconciliation efforts aimed at weakening the insurgency and fostering a sustainable peace.

Ultimately, Canada became one of the world's top donors to Afghanistan and the country was the largest single recipient of Canadian bi-lateral aid.

Throughout its time in Kandahar, the Canadian-led KPRT team focused on three signature projects: repairing the Dahla Dam and irrigation system; building and repairing 50 schools; and, finally, eradicating disease by providing 400,000 polio vaccinations to the citizens of Kandahar.

Canada was not alone in its efforts – there were 27 PRTs in Afghanistan led by coalition and NATO partners. Each one was unique. reflecting both the values of the country leading it and the needs of the Afghan people it served. The Canadian-led KPRT completed over 500 humanitarian and aid projects, despite facing continuing attacks from the Taliban resulting in several casualties.

In 2010, after managing the KPRT for 5 years, Canada prepared to turn the responsibilities over to the Americans. In 2010 Canada's senior civilian in Kandahar took on the role of Deputy Director of the KPRT while the role of Director went to the senior US representative.

At the same time, Camp Nathan Smith became the home of a detachment of ISAF Regional Command (South) Headquarters, U.S. military forces and a U.S. Army military police unit that worked with the Afghan Security Forces. In mid-July 2010, American forces took control of Kandahar City and, in August 2010, management of Camp Nathan Smith was turned over to the Americans. The KPRT continued to focus on Canada's priorities and signature projects.

The Canadian PRT would not see the end of many of the projects it started but it would leave Afghanistan knowing they had made a real difference in the lives of many Afghans.

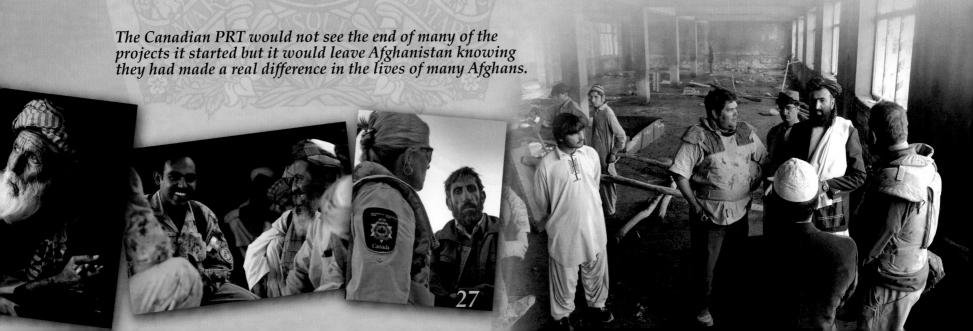

DON'T TAKE A KNIFE TO A GUN FIGHT...

In December of 2006, despite the best efforts of the Canadian troops in the region, the Taliban were still active in the Panjwaii and Zhari districts of Kandahar.

It was clear that another major operation would be necessary if the people in the area were to return to any kind of a normal life. To reduce the potential civilian casualties in such an operation, Canadian soldiers engaged in *shuras* (meetings) with tribal elders to gain their understanding and support.

The night before one of these shuras, Canadian soldiers on patrol spotted two Taliban fighters burying landmines near the meeting spot. They were quickly dispatched by the Canadians. The Canadian Military Engineers – Explosive Ordnance Disposal (CME EOD) specialists were brought in to clear the area of landmines.

Unfortunately, the engineers missed one of the mines and a Canadian soldier from the Royal 22nd Regiment (R22eR) – working with the KPRT - stepped on it, losing a foot. Operation FALCON SUMMIT claimed its first Canadian casualty.

Just 10 days before Christmas, on 15 December 2006, Op FALCON SUMMIT was launched to once again disrupt the activities of the enemy. The heavy lifting would be done by the Van Doos, operating from Forward Operating Bases (FOBs) established in the aftermath of Op MOUNTAIN THRUST and Op MEDUSA.

A day prior, it was clear that something was up as there was an increased tempo of activity at both the British bases and Canadian FOBs. The Canadians were preparing their effective but aging Leopard C2 tanks for battle. Because of their heavy armour and mobility, the Leopards were a game changer for the Canadians in Afghanistan. For the insurgents, the tanks were just too much to deal with. (When the C2s were replaced by the highly sophisticated Leopard 2A6M a year later, the field tilted even more to the Canadians' advantage.)

The primary target of Op FALCON SUMMIT was a Taliban command post that had been built and reinforced with stone, concrete and sheet metal. Very early in the morning of December 15th, NATO planes attacked and destroyed the post in a barrage of bombs, rockets and fuel air explosives.

Even as the bombs were raining down, other NATO aircraft were dropping leaflets throughout the target areas in an effort to forewarn the civilian population, encouraging them to evacuate the area and stop supporting the Taliban. They also dropped a separate leaflet directed at Taliban fighters warning of the impending battle.

On 19 December, Canadian artillery and armour opened fire in a 45 minute heavy barrage aimed at enemy installations. This 'fire for effect', along with heavy machinegun support, removed about 60 Taliban insurgents from the equation.

Just as the M777 howitzers quieted, the Canadian and ANA convoys moved out, quickly establishing new positions well forward of where they had been the day before. Outside the village of Howz-e-Madad the Canadians stopped just short of overrunning the village, in the hope of convincing the elders to give up the 900 Taliban fighters hiding within their community.

The Taliban were well protected by the thick mud walls and a rat maze of passageways throughout the village. That said, the Canadians still had an advantage. While the village provided protection, it also made it impossible for the Taliban to retreat!

After Op MEDUSA, the Canadians had built a new route summit near the Arghandab River – which they controlled. Ten kilometers to the south of Howz-e-Madad, were American soldiers, laying in wait to intercept anyone who fled in their direction. Additionally, the configuration of the village made it impossible for the enemy to maintain coordinated defences.

Experiencing little or no resistance from the Taliban over the next few days, the Canadians took control of several towns in the region. Canadian commanders credited this success to the shuras with the village leaders and the leaflet campaign.

It was not all easy. On 5 January 2007, the Van Doos were just south of Howz-e-Madad in the village of Lacookhal, scouring the village for weapons caches and insurgents. A patrol of twenty Canadian soldiers came under small arms and RPG fire from a small but determined attack force. When the smoke cleared, two of the enemy were dead and the Canadians escaped unharmed.

The next day, the battle group returned – this time supported by US helicopter gunships - and drove the enemy from the immediate area.

Op FALCON SUMMIT would not be the end of the Taliban in the region - but the end was in sight.

....TIME TO CLEAN HOUSE!

In May of 2007, the Canadians, supported by the Afghan National Army and Portuguese Special Forces (PSF), were again heading into the villages of the Zhari District. The target was the 300 Taliban fighters believed to be hiding among the population. The operation was code named Op HOOVER.

Early in the morning of 24 May 2007, the newly acquired and deadly accurate M777 howitzers of the 2 RCHA began firing at the suspected terrorist targets, far in the distance. Even as the guns were firing, the Leopard tanks of the LdSH(RC) (Strathcona's) were advancing to engage the enemy. One of the tanks hit a well-hidden landmine but there were no casualties and the Strathconas continued to move forward.

Following the tanks of the Strathcona's were contingents of the ANA (with embedded OMLT teams), riding in light pick-up trucks with mounted machine guns. By now, the Afghans, trained by NATO troops, were starting to jell as a fighting force. Those trained by the Canadian troops took a special pride in their newfound skills and were showing signs of becoming professional soldiers. What no one could doubt was their bravery and sense of resolve as they fought to take their country back from the Taliban.

As British fighter aircraft roared overhead, Portuguese commanders, along with their PSF snipers, were neutralizing a number of enemy positions to the west of the Canadians. Despite stiff enemy resistance, the Portuguese fought hard and were successful in their mission. Only one of their soldiers had to be medevac'd for treatment.

While all this was happening, the 2 RCR BG was massing just north of the Arghandab River. They were the anvil. As the enemy tried to escape, they would move ahead of the hammer – the Strathcona's and the Afghans – and run straight into the waiting sights of the RCRs. This tactical manoeuvre proved to be an effective and devastating trap to the Taliban.

As the battle was unfolding, tragedy struck. Corporal Matthew McCully, a signals operator with the Canadian team mentoring the ANA, was killed by a land mine just outside Nalgham village while another Canadian soldier and an Afghan translator were wounded.

The next day the battle was declared over with reports of between 60 and 100 Taliban fighters killed. Militarily, it had been a success; however, it would be up to the CIMIC teams to solidify that success by establishing a working relationship with the local community leaders.

The only way they could hope to keep the Taliban at bay was to help the community get back on its feet as quickly as possible, by providing a source of clean water, health clinics, schools for the children and a sense of security for the townspeople. It was not an easy sell!

85 DAYS OF HELL...IN HELMAND

In March of 2007, Canadian Leopard tanks, LAV-3 light armored vehicles and infantry had been patrolling western Kandahar province in support of NATO's Op ACHILLES – the largest NATO operation to date. However, the RCR Battle Group was on stand-by to throw its full force into the battle.

Throughout the winter of 2006 and into 2007, thousands of Taliban fighters had moved into the area of northern Helmand province. Afghanistan's inhospitable weather makes fighting a winter campaign very difficult, so the Taliban tradition was to build up its strength in the winter and attack in the spring.

However, this time it was different. The British, responsible for the overall security of Helmand province, had been engaged in a succession of skirmishes and battles with the enemy throughout January and February 2007. Leading NATO forces, the UK troops had seen action in the Kajaki and Sangin districts and had engaged and killed 15 Taliban during Op KRYPTONITE in January.

As a result of the pressure from the British, the Taliban did not feel confident enough to directly engage NATO forces - so turned to sniping, IEDs and acts of terrorism. It was evident that the Taliban were not planning to wait for the traditional spring military campaign.

In response, NATO announced on 6 March 2007 that ISAF had (at 5:00 am) launched Op ACHILLES, involving two brigades comprized of troops from U.S., British, Afghan, Dutch and Canadian units. Ultimately, 4500 NATO troops and 1000 Afghan National Security Forces personnel would engage the enemy.

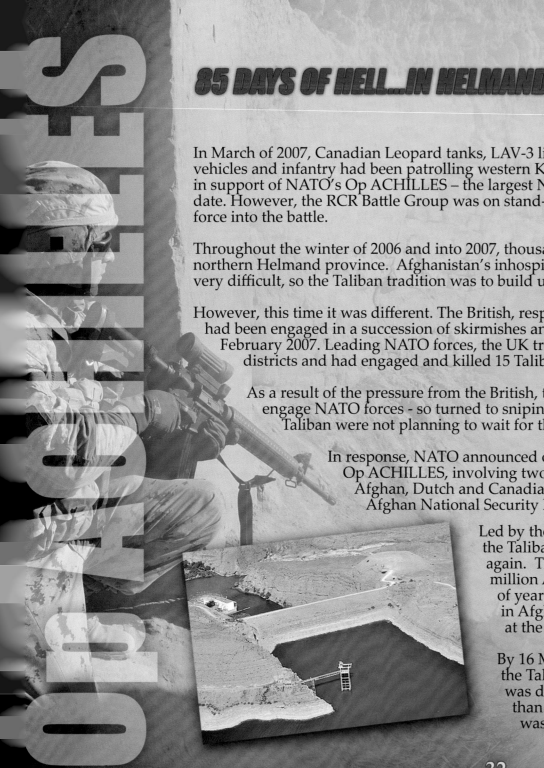

Led by the British, Op ACHILLES was focused on suppressing the Taliban in and around the Kajakai Dam and getting it operating again. The dam had the capacity to provide power for over 2 million Afghans but had not been in operation for a number of years. This was one of 14,000 PRT reconstruction projects in Afghanistan. ISAF was determined to install a new turbine at the dam and get the local communities back on the grid.

By 16 March, NATO reported that its troops were engaging the Taliban across southern Afghanistan but that the enemy was doing its best to avoid ISAF – often sliding away rather than fighting. When the Taliban did stand its ground, it was firmly defeated with few or no ISAF casualties.

Canadian BGen Tim Grant ordered the 2 RCR Battle Group into the fray on the morning of 5 April 2007 under code name Op SILVER. The Canadians were moving up to support the British and Afghan forces fighting in the Sangin Valley - providing additional force protection.

Speaking to the media, a Canadian army spokesperson said that, while they were moving forward, the Canadians were not in real danger of being engaged by the enemy. What did worry the Canadian soldiers was the very real risk of IEDs – a ubiquitous threat throughout the area.

In the worst single incident of Op ACHILLES, six Canadians were killed on 8 April 2007, when their vehicle was destroyed by a roadside bomb in Western Kandahar.

Op ACHILLES continued, with ISAF making substantial gains. On 30 April, the Brit led ISAF force of 1000, supported by ANA troops, fought in the Sangin Valley, pushing the enemy north and out of the village of Gereshk. Ultimately, 130 Taliban fighters were targeted and dispatched through combined ground and air operations. However, local protests broke out when it was claimed, by the Taliban, that it was not fighters who had been killed - but civilians. Angry reaction and protests broke out across the region.

The fighting continued, with ISAF chasing down the terrorists. On the 13th of May, Mullah Dadullah, the Taliban's second in command, was killed by allied forces in Helmand Province. On 18 May, air strikes destroyed a Taliban convoy, killing 14 insurgents and wounding ten. Three days later, the Taliban attempted an ambush on a US and Afghan patrol. When the haze of battle cleared, 25 insurgents had paid the ultimate price.

On 30 May 2007, ISAF declared Op ACHILLES concluded. While it had been a tactical success, the insurgency was not over. There were more fights still to come. However, the Kandahar Region was now safer for the reconstruction effort.

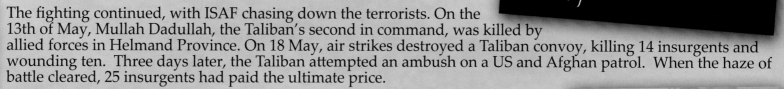

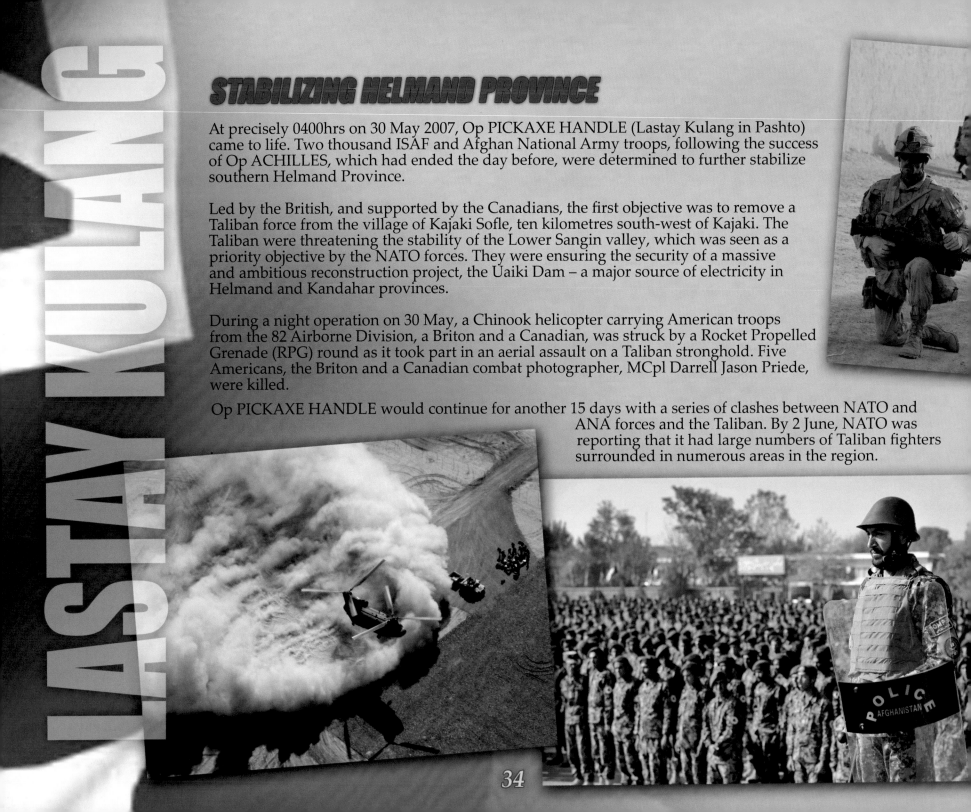

STABILIZING HELMAND PROVINCE

At precisely 0400hrs on 30 May 2007, Op PICKAXE HANDLE (Lastay Kulang in Pashto) came to life. Two thousand ISAF and Afghan National Army troops, following the success of Op ACHILLES, which had ended the day before, were determined to further stabilize southern Helmand Province.

Led by the British, and supported by the Canadians, the first objective was to remove a Taliban force from the village of Kajaki Sofle, ten kilometres south-west of Kajaki. The Taliban were threatening the stability of the Lower Sangin valley, which was seen as a priority objective by the NATO forces. They were ensuring the security of a massive and ambitious reconstruction project, the Uaiki Dam – a major source of electricity in Helmand and Kandahar provinces.

During a night operation on 30 May, a Chinook helicopter carrying American troops from the 82 Airborne Division, a Briton and a Canadian, was struck by a Rocket Propelled Grenade (RPG) round as it took part in an aerial assault on a Taliban stronghold. Five Americans, the Briton and a Canadian combat photographer, MCpl Darrell Jason Priede, were killed.

Op PICKAXE HANDLE would continue for another 15 days with a series of clashes between NATO and ANA forces and the Taliban. By 2 June, NATO was reporting that it had large numbers of Taliban fighters surrounded in numerous areas in the region.

At the same time, the sappers from the Royal Engineers (British Army) were starting to work on various reconstruction projects to help the villagers of the region return to a normal life.

However, no one could claim the region was safe. On 5 June, NATO again engaged the Taliban with ground and air forces killing approximately 25 of the enemy in Southern Afghanistan. A bloody gun battle and air strikes killed an estimated two dozen Taliban fighters in Southern Afghanistan, the U.S.-led coalition and Afghan government reported.

On 6 June a British soldier was killed at a Taliban position north-east of Gereshk, while another NATO soldier was also killed in the south.

During the same period, 80 Taliban fighters drowned trying to cross the Helmand River in makeshift boats in two different incidents. The boats sank on their own but the drownings were witnessed by NATO helicopters. It was a telling blow against the Taliban.

As Op PICKAXE HANDLE drew to a close, NATO declared victory. Sangin and Gereshk were Taliban-free and a new governor was in control. However, the Taliban contradicted that claim. It became clear that the battle for Helmand Province was not over!

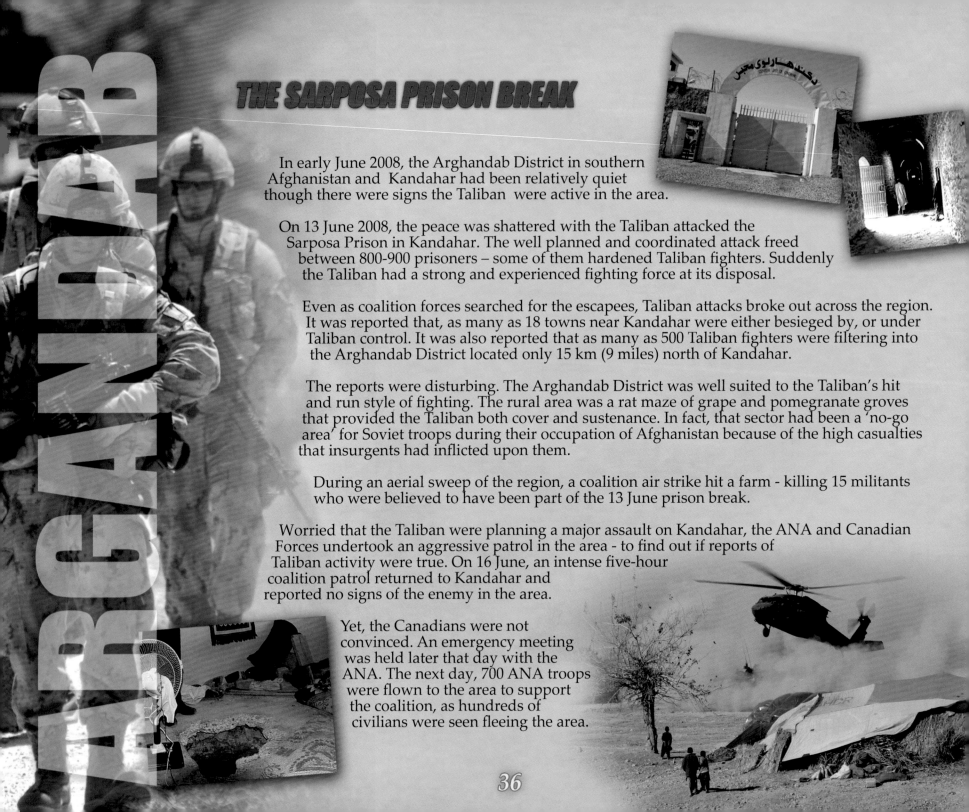

THE SARPOSA PRISON BREAK

In early June 2008, the Arghandab District in southern Afghanistan and Kandahar had been relatively quiet though there were signs the Taliban were active in the area.

On 13 June 2008, the peace was shattered with the Taliban attacked the Sarposa Prison in Kandahar. The well planned and coordinated attack freed between 800-900 prisoners – some of them hardened Taliban fighters. Suddenly the Taliban had a strong and experienced fighting force at its disposal.

Even as coalition forces searched for the escapees, Taliban attacks broke out across the region. It was reported that, as many as 18 towns near Kandahar were either besieged by, or under Taliban control. It was also reported that as many as 500 Taliban fighters were filtering into the Arghandab District located only 15 km (9 miles) north of Kandahar.

The reports were disturbing. The Arghandab District was well suited to the Taliban's hit and run style of fighting. The rural area was a rat maze of grape and pomegranate groves that provided the Taliban both cover and sustenance. In fact, that sector had been a 'no-go area' for Soviet troops during their occupation of Afghanistan because of the high casualties that insurgents had inflicted upon them.

During an aerial sweep of the region, a coalition air strike hit a farm - killing 15 militants who were believed to have been part of the 13 June prison break.

Worried that the Taliban were planning a major assault on Kandahar, the ANA and Canadian Forces undertook an aggressive patrol in the area - to find out if reports of Taliban activity were true. On 16 June, an intense five-hour coalition patrol returned to Kandahar and reported no signs of the enemy in the area.

Yet, the Canadians were not convinced. An emergency meeting was held later that day with the ANA. The next day, 700 ANA troops were flown to the area to support the coalition, as hundreds of civilians were seen fleeing the area.

On the evening of 17 June, it was abundantly clear that a battle was brewing. The Taliban engaged a group of Canadian soldiers in a small intense firefight while other Taliban fighters were destroying culverts and bridges around Kandahar and moving arms and ammunition into place.

The Canadians quickly responded by increasing the defenses at the local power plant, the Governor's residence and their own camp.

The Taliban were no longer hiding their presence – or their intentions. Akhatar Mohammad, an escapee from Sarposa Prison, was publicly proclaiming that he was personally leading 200 insurgents ready to enter Arghandab. Taliban commander Mullah Ahmedullah was reported to say that all the Taliban was waiting for - was the coalition forces to make the first move.

That first move came on the morning of 18 June 2008. ANA and Canadian forces attacked known militant positions throughout the region. Despite the preparations made by the Taliban, the Canadians and ANA met only pockets of resistance. The village of Talin was hit by an airstrike killing 20 insurgents. In Khohak 16 insurgents were killed in a firefight with the ANA that cost two Afghan soldiers their lives.

By 19 June, BGen Denis Thompson declared the Taliban defeated - and Kandahar firmly in coalition control. He did warn, however, that the Taliban could regroup and return. Altogether 96 Taliban fighters were killed in the Battle of Arghandab, thankfully, there no Canadian casualties or losses.

"Keep your families safe. When there is fighting near your home, stay inside while ANSF defeat the enemies of Afghanistan."

—Leaflet dropped over Arghandab

LEAVING AFGHANISTAN - A BETTER PLACE

On 12 March 2010, General Walt Natynczyk told the troops that the end of the largest deployment of Canadian troops since the Second World War was drawing to a close. Over 40,000 Canadian Forces personnel had served in Afghanistan. General Natynczyk was certainly no stranger to the men and women in theatre. An extraordinary leader, he replaced Gen Hillier as CDS in July 2008.

The cost had been high: 158 soldiers, one reporter, one diplomat and two civilian accountants had been killed. Hundreds more had been wounded. The battles, patrols, IEDs and the enemy had taken their toll. Yet, Canada's success in Afghanistan cannot be calculated in military victories alone. The courage and compassion of Canadians, both military and civilian, in Afghanistan made a very real difference to the lives of ordinary Afghans.

In 2005, at the request of Afghan President Karzai, LGen Rick Hillier provided senior military officers to advise the Afghan government. The officers served as part of the Strategic Advisory Team (SAT) alongside Canadian Embassy and Department of Foreign Affairs planners.

When the Canadians deployed to the Kandahar and to KPRT Camp Nathan Smith, more improvements followed. New methods of "counter-insurgency strategy, counter-IED, intelligence and surveillance and the ability to integrate and synchronize efforts with other government departments and agencies" were developed.

In the Dand, Arghandab, Panjwaii, and Zhari districts of Kandahar province, security and stability greatly increased over the time the Canadians served there. More and more Afghan troops worked with the Canadians, learning how to be better soldiers and preparing for the day when the Canadian troops would leave for the last time.

Afghan civilians benefited from the Canadian presence at KAF as well. In addition to treating Canadian and allied wounded solders, the Canadians working at the Role III medical facility at KAF saved the lives of Afghan citizens injured in the conflict.

The KPRT worked hard to improve the lives of Afghans in the city - by focusing on governance, security and development. Paved roads, build by the KPRT, allowed the Afghan government to deliver vital aid to remote areas and allowed farmers to bring their produce to market. The 50 schools expanded or repaired by the Canadians meant thousands of children could get an education.

The Legacy

In July 2011, Canada officially ceased its military operations to return to Kabul. Building on the lessons learned since the conflict began in 2001, almost 1000 Canadians were assigned to assist the NATO Training Mission – Afghanistan (NTM-A).

The Canadian contribution to the NTM-A was the second largest of all the countries participating. Soon the Afghan National Army and the Afghan Air Force were all learning alongside the members of the Canadian Armed Forces. More than 160 Afghan Kandaks (battalion-sized units) would benefit from Canadian skills and expertise. The police training detainment management for the Afghanistan National Police was provided by a select number of Canadians from the RCMP, several municipal police forces across the country as well as Foreign Affairs and Correctional Services Canada.

Continuing the legacy of the Role III health-care facility in Kandahar, Canadian Forces providers worked as advisors/mentors to the Afghan Armed Force Academy of Medical Sciences (AFAMS) in Kabul, which was soon to be recognized world-wide as a centre of heath-care excellence.

Canada, of course, did not do it alone, but was part of a large international coalition. Nonetheless, the numbers are impressive. While Canada was in Afghanistan, 24,000 km of roads and 75 kilometres of railway were built; power grid connectivity grew by 600%; more than 2,600 km of fibre optic cable connected major cities and; 9 million children went to more than 13,000 schools!

Perhaps the most important legacy of Canada's time in Afghanistan is the fact that the country, once ravaged by the Soviet occupation and the subsequent civil war, is once again a functioning country.

Canada oversaw the first democratic election in the country's history. The ANP and ANA, both reduced to almost irrelevant forces over 20 years, are back providing security and peace of mind to average Afghans. The men and women who serve with them are learning to be both professional and effective.

Thanks to the courage and dedication of the Canadians who served in Afghanistan, the country is once more an active member of the international community. There is a brighter future in store for the Afghan people - the opportunity to learn and prosper - where women can contribute to society, a young girl can go to school and a boy can again fly a kite in the bright Afghanistan skies - and dream.

The work in Afghanistan is not done – but the essentials are now in a place for Afghans to see it through to the end!

THE HIGHWAY OF HEROES

For those Canadians who served, and made the ultimate sacrifice in Afghanistan, their last journey was on the Highway of Heroes.

The 401, a simple stretch of highway leading from CFB Trenton to Toronto, spontaneously became a place where ordinary Canadians - men and women, young and old, veterans and civilians – came to say thank you one last time.

Thousands of kilometers away in Afghanistan, each fallen Canadian began a long journey home. A simple but moving ceremony on the tarmac at the Kandahar Air Field paid honour to each fallen hero. As the flag-draped coffin was respectfully loaded on a plane, Canadians and allies, military and civilian, lined the runway – the piper played a solemn lament.

Accompanied by comrades the fallen hero was flown thousands of miles to family and home for one last time.

Appreciating the importance of every repatriation flight, Canada's Governors General, Prime Minister and Chiefs of the Defence Staff were a familiar sight on the runway in Trenton.

As the CF aircraft began its descent into CFB Trenton north of Toronto, those on the ramp stood waiting by the black limousines and hearses – an agonizing wait which would ultimately make the unbearable real. The official word for it was 'repatriation'.

As the motorcade turned onto Highway 401, it picked up speed - taking the fallen hero to Toronto for a few formalities, then ultimately, to their place of rest. They were not going to be alone.

A tradition, uniquely Canadian, had begun with the first hero to come home. Private citizens, with no connection to those who had died in Afghanistan, came together – first on overpasses, every overpass, then lining the highway. Some stood silently, others held Canadian flags, and still others wept silently. Canada was bringing its own home.

No one had told them to be there. Canadians just knew they needed to be there. In the vastness of Canada, those who could not be on the first Highway of Heroes were soon standing on Highways of Heroes in provinces and territories from British Columbia to the Maritimes.

A war on the other side of the world had quietly brought Canadians together in a way nothing else had ever done. In a quiet unassuming way, Canadians said goodbye to their heroes.

AFTERWORD

...from Canadian Joint Operations Command

The story of our experiences in Afghanistan will be told not only by some 40,000 Canadian Armed Forces men and women and our partners who served there, but also by their families, friends, and tremendous supporters like Rod McLeod and Norman Leach who have produced this captivating book.

This book provides yet another lens through which we can reflect on and take stock of the service, sacrifices, and achievements of so many. It reminds us that this long mission was all about the people alongside, for whom, and with whom we served – our soldiers, sailors, and air personnel, our civilian and law enforcement partners, our international and Afghan teammates in the mission, our families at home, and our fellow Canadians who supported us in ways we could never have predicted or imagined. Those we see in these pictures, and all those with whom they served, did so with distinction, incredible determination, selfless teamwork, and profound courage.

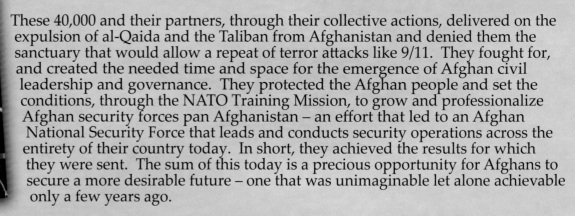

These 40,000 and their partners, through their collective actions, delivered on the expulsion of al-Qaida and the Taliban from Afghanistan and denied them the sanctuary that would allow a repeat of terror attacks like 9/11. They fought for, and created the needed time and space for the emergence of Afghan civil leadership and governance. They protected the Afghan people and set the conditions, through the NATO Training Mission, to grow and professionalize Afghan security forces pan Afghanistan – an effort that led to an Afghan National Security Force that leads and conducts security operations across the entirety of their country today. In short, they achieved the results for which they were sent. The sum of this today is a precious opportunity for Afghans to secure a more desirable future – one that was unimaginable let alone achievable only a few years ago.

Our experiences, accomplishments, and sacrifices had a profound impact on our military and families at home. We honour and commemorate our fallen, we are and continue to improve our care for our wounded, we have captured best practises relevant to the types of security challenges we see today and anticipate in the future, and we are recognized as a first class professional fighting force – serving and ready to serve Canadians wherever required.

This mission has been seminal in our relationship as Canadians with our military. From yellow ribbons, to community memorials, to memorial highways, to highway of heroes, to Soldier On and the Military Families Fund and countless other examples, Canadians have truly supported their military and continue to do so. We are comforted, sustained, and inspired by all of this.

On 12 March 2014, our Chief of the Defence Staff presided over the lowering of the Canadian Flag at the International Security Assistance Force HQ in Kabul, marking the end of our 12 year military contribution to the incredible multi-national effort. He thanked our operational partners, encouraged Afghans to persist, and highlighted Canada's continued multi-year commitment to the Afghanistan National Development Strategy that is still being championed through Canada's Embassy team there.

The Canadian Armed Forces contribution to the mission in Afghanistan is concluded. Afghans and their international mission partners – including Canada's diplomatic mission in Kabul – are pressing on.

Lieutenant-General Stuart Beare, CMM, CSM, MSM, CD
Commander, Canadian Joint Operations Command
Oct 2012 to July 2014

National Day May 9, 2014
of HONOUR
PROGRAMME

Canada

NATIONAL DA

OF HONOUR

AFGHANISTAN MEMORIAL VIGIL

After the first four Canadians were killed in Afghanistan, at the Tarnak Farm incident, it soon became clear that the DND would have to find a way to deal with the commemoration of those who gave their lives in the line of duty. Until this unfortunate event, nobody had really given it much thought.

AFPP International, a Calgary based company, had been actively engaged in the design and production of military awards and imprinted sportswear since 1988. As its founder (and a serving soldier), I had spent enough time in uniform to learn the nuances of military life and culture, and had a good understanding of the CAF and how it functioned.

Recognizing the pressing need for appropriate recognition, I set to the task of designing and producing a laser engraved granite plaque as a suitable tribute to the fallen servicemen. Much of it had to be photo shopped because, while all four were qualified infanteers and paratroopers, only Sgt Leger was properly attired. The only available pictures of Privates Smith and Green in uniform were from Basic Training, and the photo of Private Dyer in civilian clothing. After considerable photographic reconstruction, two of the resulting plaques were presented to LFWA Headquarters and PPCLI Regimental Headquarters in Edmonton and a third was sent to Kabul to be mounted on a stone beside the parade square in Camp Julien.

Eighteen months would pass until Sgt Short and Cpl Beerenfenger from 3 RCR would fall victim to an IED. A mere 3 months later, Cpl Jamie Murphy was killed by a suicide bomber. In November 2004, as the Canadians were relocating to the new camp in Kandahar, Pte. Woodfield (2 RCR) was killed.

As the camp was being established in KAF, a special area was set aside behind the headquarters building for a proper cenotaph. In time, soldiers would stop by to remember a fallen comrade or simply for a moment of solitude. The engineers took special pride in the design and construction of the new memorial. Every day, the memorial was caringly cleaned and maintained. It would eventually represent all the fallen soldiers under Canadian command.

While uniformity is a big part of military culture, each plaque is a little different, reflecting the individuality of each of the fallen heroes. The plaques were designed by Rod McLeod of AFPP-International and engraved by Sheldon Fedechko of Laser Etch Technologies Ltd. in Calgary, Alberta.

As the Canadian assets were being carefully gathered, cataloged and packed into sea cans for the return to Canada, the engineers dismantled and crated the entire structure. Each plaque was painstakingly wrapped and boxed for the long journey home.

An effective mobile display unit was developed to enable the collection of memorial plaques to travel the length and breadth of Canada, allowing Canadians to visit the monument - and pay their last respects to the brave men and women who gave their lives in the line of duty.

On 9 May 2014, to mark the National Day of Honour, the display was officially introduced to the public on Parliament Hill. A few days later, it travelled to the Canadian Embassy in Washington DC before it began a 6 month journey to all the major cities and military bases across the country. .

Ultimately, it will come to rest in the Nation's Capital, in a location that will enable Canadians to visit and pay homage to our fallen.

All those who touched this project can forever take pride in the fact that they are now part of a great Canadian legacy.

Chief of the Defence Staff, General Tom Lawson is accompanied by The Honourable Peter MacKay, then Minister of National Defence for the unveiling of the Afghanistan Vilgil Memorial - 8 July 2013

47

OP APOLLO — 3rd Battalion Princess Patricia's Canadian Light Infantry. Sgt. Marc D. Leger, Pte. Ainsworth Dyer, Pte. Richard Green, Pte. Nathan L. Smith. 17/04/02

"A man clearly dedicated to the ideals of freedom and making this a better world in which to live." Mr. Glyn R. Berry — Political Director, Provincial Reconstruction Team, Foreign Affairs Canada. 14 Jun 1946 – 15 Jan 2006

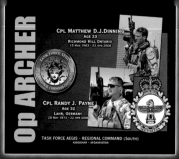

Op ARCHER — Cpl Matthew D.J. Dinning, Age 23, Richmond Hill Ontario, 15 Mar 1983 – 22 Apr 2006. Cpl Randy J. Payne, Age 32, Lahr, Germany, 29 May 1973 – 22 Apr 2006. TASK FORCE AEGIS - REGIONAL COMMAND (South), KANDAHAR - AFGHANISTAN

Op ARCHER — Sgt Vaughan Ingram, Age 35, Burgeo, NF, 11 Jun 1971 – 3 Aug 2006. Cpl Christopher Reid, Age 34, Truro, NS, 21 Sep 1971 – 3 Aug 2006. Cpl Bryce J. Keller, Age 27, Regina, SK, 27 May 1979 – 3 Aug 2006. Pte Kevin Dallaire, Age 22, Calgary, AB, 23 Sep 1983 – 3 Aug 2006. TASK FORCE ORION - REGIONAL COMMAND (South), 1st Battalion - Princess Patricia's Canadian Light Infantry, KANDAHAR - AFGHANISTAN

TASK FORCE AFGHANISTAN — R-2, Cpl David Robert Braun, Age 27, Born: Raymore, SK, 03 May 1979 – 22 Aug 2006. 2ND BN - PRINCESS PATRICIA'S CANADIAN LIGHT INFANTRY. TASK FORCE 3-06, 1ST BATTALION - THE ROYAL CANADIAN REGIMENT, KANDAHAR - AFGHANISTAN

OP ATHENA - ROTO 0. 02/10/03. Sgt R.A. Short, Cpl R.C. Beerenfenger. 3RD BATTALION THE ROYAL CANADIAN REGIMENT BATTALION GROUP

Op ARCHER — MCpl Timothy Wilson, Age 30, Grande Prairie, AB, 25 Jul 1975 – 4 Mar 2006. Corporal Paul Davis, Age 28, Bridgewater, N.S., 16 Nov 1977 – 2 Mar 2006. 1 PPCLI BATTLE GROUP (TF ORION), KANDAHAR - AFGHANISTAN

Op ARCHER — Capt Nichola K.S. Goddard, Age 26, Born in Madang, Papua New Guinea, 2 May 1980 – 17 May 2006. 1 ROYAL CANADIAN HORSE ARTILLERY (A BATTERY) - TASK FORCE ORION, KANDAHAR - AFGHANISTAN

Op ARCHER — MCpl Raymond F. Arndt, Age 31, Born: Norton, AB, 20 Nov 1974 – 30 Aug 2006. THE LOYAL EDMONTON REGIMENT, NATIONAL SUPPORT ELEMENT, KANDAHAR - AFGHANISTAN

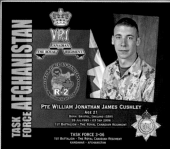

TASK FORCE AFGHANISTAN — R-2, Pte William Jonathan James Cushley, Age 21, Born: Bristol, England (GBR), 28 Jul 1985 – 03 Sep 2006. 1ST BATTALION - THE ROYAL CANADIAN REGIMENT, TASK FORCE 3-06, KANDAHAR - AFGHANISTAN

OP ATHENA — Cpl Jamie B. Murphy, 08 July 1977 – 27 Jan 2004. 3RD BN. THE ROYAL CANADIAN REGIMENT BATTALION GROUP - ROTO 0

Op ARCHER — Private Robert H. Costall, Age 22, Thunder Bay, ON, 27 Sep 1983 – 29 Mar 2006. 1 PPCLI BATTLE GROUP (TF ORION), KANDAHAR - AFGHANISTAN

Op ARCHER — Cpl Anthony Joseph Boneca, Age 21, Born: Thunder Bay, ON, 13 Feb 1985 – 00 Jul 2006. THE LAKE SUPERIOR SCOTTISH REGIMENT, 1 PRINCESS PATRICIA'S CANADIAN LIGHT INFANTRY - TASK FORCE ORION, KANDAHAR - AFGHANISTAN

TASK FORCE AFGHANISTAN — R-2, MCpl Jeffrey Scott Walsh, Age 33, Born: Saskatoon, SK, 07 Aug 1973 – 09 Aug 2006. 2ND BN - PRINCESS PATRICIA'S CANADIAN LIGHT INFANTRY. TASK FORCE 3-06, 1ST BATTALION - THE ROYAL CANADIAN REGIMENT, KANDAHAR - AFGHANISTAN

TASK FORCE AFGHANISTAN — R-2, WO Frank Robert Mellish, Age 38, Born: Truro, Nova Scotia, 10 Feb 1968 – 03 Sep 2006. 1ST BATTALION - THE ROYAL CANADIAN REGIMENT, TASK FORCE 3-06, KANDAHAR - AFGHANISTAN

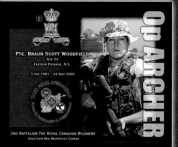

Op ARCHER — Pte. Braun Scott Woodfield, Age 24, Eastern Passage, N.S., 3 Jan 1981 – 24 Nov 2005. 2ND BATTALION THE ROYAL CANADIAN REGIMENT, GAGETOWN NEW BRUNSWICK CANADA

Op ARCHER — Bdr. Myles S.J. Mansell, Age 25, Victoria, British Columbia, 5 Aug 1982 – 22 Apr 2006, 5TH FIELD BATTERY RCA. Lt. William Turner, Age 45, Toronto, Ontario, 13 June 1961 – 22 Apr 2006, 20 Fd Regt RCA - Edmonton, AB. TASK FORCE AEGIS - REGIONAL COMMAND (South), KANDAHAR - AFGHANISTAN

Op ARCHER — Cpl Jason Patrick Warren, Age 29, Quebec City, QC, 17 Oct 1978 – 22 Jul 2006, THE BLACK WATCH (ROYAL HIGHLAND REGIMENT) OF CANADA. Cpl Francisco Oliver Gomez, Age 44, Venezuela, 23 May 1962 – 22 Jul 2006, 1ST BATTALION - PRINCESS PATRICIA'S CANADIAN LIGHT INFANTRY. TASK FORCE ORION - REGIONAL COMMAND (South), KANDAHAR - AFGHANISTAN

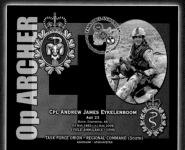

Op ARCHER — Cpl Andrew James Eykelenboom, Age 23, Born: Edmonton, AB, 30 Nov 1982 – 11 Aug 2006. 1 FIELD AMBULANCE - CFHS, TASK FORCE ORION - REGIONAL COMMAND (South), KANDAHAR - AFGHANISTAN

TASK FORCE AFGHANISTAN — R-2, WO Richard Francis Nolan, Age 39, Born: St. John's, Newfoundland, 27 May 1967 – 03 Sep 2006. 1ST BATTALION - THE ROYAL CANADIAN REGIMENT, TASK FORCE 3-06, KANDAHAR - AFGHANISTAN

Sgt Shane Hank Stachnik
Age 30
Born: Edmonton, Alberta
13 Nov 1975 - 03 Sep 2006
2 Combat Engineer Regiment
TASK FORCE 3-06
1st Battalion - The Royal Canadian Regiment
Kandahar - Afghanistan

Cpl Shane Patrick Keating
Age 30
Born: Estevan, SK
17 Dec 1975 - 18 Sep 2006
2nd Bn - Princess Patricia's Canadian Light Infantry - Shilo
TASK FORCE 3-06
1st Battalion - The Royal Canadian Regiment

Cpl Robert Thomas James Mitchell
Age 32
Born: Owen Sound, ON
19 Dec 1973 - 3 Oct 2006
The Royal Canadian Dragoons - Petawawa
TASK FORCE 3-06
1st Battalion - The Royal Canadian Regiment
Kandahar - Afghanistan

CWO Robert Michel Joseph Girouard
Age 46
Born: Bouctouche New Brunswick
25 Nov 1960 - 27 Nov 2006
1st Battalion - The Royal Canadian Regiment
TASK FORCE - Battle Group RSM
Kandahar - Afghanistan

Pte Kevin Vincent Kennedy
Age 20
Born: St. John's, Newfoundland
20 Oct 1986 - 8 Apr 2007
2nd Battalion - The Royal Canadian Regiment
2 RCR BG, H Coy
Kandahar - Afghanistan

Pte Mark Anthony Graham
Age 33
Born: Gordon Town, Jamaica
17 May 1973 - 04 Sep 2006
1st Battalion - The Royal Canadian Regiment
TASK FORCE 3-06
1st Battalion - The Royal Canadian Regiment

Cpl Keith Ian Morley
Age 30
Born: Winnipeg, MB
23 Sep 1975 - 18 Sep 2006
2nd Bn - Princess Patricia's Canadian Light Infantry - Shilo
TASK FORCE 3-06
1st Battalion - The Royal Canadian Regiment

Tpr Mark Andrew Wilson
Age 39
Born: London, On
15 Dec 1966 - 07 Oct 2006
The Royal Canadian Dragoons - Petawawa
TASK FORCE 3-06
1st Battalion - The Royal Canadian Regiment

Cpl Albert Hugh Storm
Age 36
Born: Niagara Falls, Ontario
1 Feb 1970 - 27 Nov 2006
1st Battalion - The Royal Canadian Regiment
TASK FORCE 3-06
1st Battalion - The Royal Canadian Regiment

Sgt Donald Jason Lucas
Age 31
Born: St. John's, Newfoundland
20 Feb 1976 - 8 Apr 2007
2nd Battalion - The Royal Canadian Regiment
2 RCR BG, H Coy
Kandahar - Afghanistan

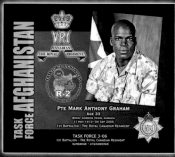
Cpl Glen Harold Arnold
Age 32
Born: Sudbury, ON
4 Jun 1974 - 18 Sep 2006
2 Field Ambulance, Petawawa
TASK FORCE 3-06
1st Battalion - The Royal Canadian Regiment
Kandahar - Afghanistan

Pte Joshua James Klukie
Age 23
Born: Thunder Bay, Ontario
16 Feb 1983 - 29 Sep 2006
1st Battalion - The Royal Canadian Regiment
TASK FORCE 3-06
1st Battalion - The Royal Canadian Regiment

Sgt Darcy Scott Tedford
Age 32
Born: Calgary, Alberta
12 Aug 1974 - 14 Oct 2006
1st Battalion - The Royal Canadian Regiment
TASK FORCE 3-06
1st Battalion - The Royal Canadian Regiment

Cpl Ronald Kevin Megeney
Age 25
Born: New Glasgow, NS
18 Jan 1982 - 06 Mar 2007
1st Bn Nova Scotia Highlanders
NSE Force Protection
Kandahar - Afghanistan

Cpl Brent Donald Poland
Age 37
Born: Sarnia, Ontario
26 Oct 1969 - 8 Apr 2007
2nd Battalion - The Royal Canadian Regiment
2 RCR BG, H Coy
Kandahar - Afghanistan

Pte David Robert James Byers
Age 22
Born: Espanola, ON
26 May 1984 - 18 Sep 2006
2nd Bn - Princess Patricia's Canadian Light Infantry - Shilo
TASK FORCE 3-06
1st Battalion - The Royal Canadian Regiment
Kandahar - Afghanistan

Sgt Craig Paul Gillam
Age 40
Born: Stephenville Crossing, NF
20 Apr 1966 - 3 Oct 2006
The Royal Canadian Dragoons - Petawawa
TASK FORCE 3-06
1st Battalion - The Royal Canadian Regiment
Kandahar - Afghanistan

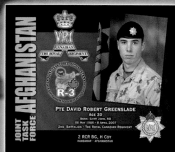
Pte Blake Neil Williamson
Age 23
Born: Hamilton, Ontario
25 Jan 1983 - 14 Oct 2006
1st Battalion - The Royal Canadian Regiment
TASK FORCE 3-06
1st Battalion - The Royal Canadian Regiment

Pte David Robert Greenslade
Age 20
Born: Saint John, NB
06 May 1986 - 8 Apr 2007
2nd Battalion - The Royal Canadian Regiment
2 RCR BG, H Coy
Kandahar - Afghanistan

Cpl Christopher Paul Raymond Stannix
Age 24
Born: North Bay, Ontario
11 Jun 1982 - 8 Apr 2007
Princess Louise Fusiliers, Halifax, Nova Scotia
2 RCR BG, H Coy
Kandahar - Afghanistan

JOINT TASK FORCE AFGHANISTAN — R-3
CPL AARON EDWARD WILLIAMS
AGE 23
BORN: PERTH-ANDOVER, NEW BRUNSWICK
8 OCT 1983 - 8 APR 2007
2ND BATTALION - THE ROYAL CANADIAN REGIMENT
2 RCR BG, H COY
KANDAHAR - AFGHANISTAN

JOINT TASK FORCE AFGHANISTAN — R-3
CPL MATTHEW JONATHAN CEDRIC MCCULLY
AGE 25
BORN: YORK, ONTARIO
11 APRIL 1982 - 25 MAY 2007
2 CMBG HQ & SIG SQN
OPERATIONAL MENTORING AND LIAISON TEAM
KANDAHAR - AFGHANISTAN

TASK FORCE AFGHANISTAN — R-3
SGT CHRISTOS KARIGIANNIS
AGE 31
BORN: MONTREAL, QC
20 SEP 1975 - 20 JUN 2007
3RD BN - PRINCESS PATRICIA'S CANADIAN LIGHT INFANTRY
2 RCR BG - C COY
KANDAHAR - AFGHANISTAN
VP

TASK FORCE AFGHANISTAN — R-3
MCPL COLIN STUART FRANCIS BASON
AGE 28
BORN: BURNABY, BC
13 DEC 1978 - 4 JUL 2007
THE ROYAL WESTMINSTER REGIMENT - NEW WESTMINSTER
2 RCR BG - C COY
KANDAHAR - AFGHANISTAN

ROTO 4 AFGHANISTAN — R4
SDT SIMON JMSS LONGTIN
ÂGE 23
NÉ À LONGUEUIL, QC
2 NOVEMBRE 1983 AU 19 AOÛT 2007
3E BATAILLON ROYAL 22E RÉGIMENT VALCARTIER
GROUPEMENT TACTIQUE
3E BATAILLON ROYAL 22E RÉGIMENT
KANDAHAR - AFGHANISTAN

JOINT TASK FORCE AFGHANISTAN — R-3
TPR PATRICK JAMES PENTLAND
AGE 23
BORN: LAHR, GERMANY
13 JUN 1984 - 11 APR 2007
THE ROYAL CANADIAN DRAGOONS - PETAWAWA
2 RCR BG, RECCE SQN
KANDAHAR - AFGHANISTAN

OP ATHENA
MCPL DARRELL JASON PRIEDE
AGE 30
BORN: BURLINGTON, ONTARIO
02 APR 1977 - 30 MAY 2007
CANADIAN FORCES IMAGERY TECHNICIAN
RC SOUTH HQ
KANDAHAR - AFGHANISTAN

TASK FORCE AFGHANISTAN — R-3
PTE JOEL VINCENT WIEBE
AGE 22
BORN: EDMONTON, AB
21 JUN 1984 - 20 JUN 2007
3RD BN - PRINCESS PATRICIA'S CANADIAN LIGHT INFANTRY - EDMONTON
2 RCR BG - C COY
KANDAHAR - AFGHANISTAN
VP

TASK FORCE AFGHANISTAN — R-3
CAPT MATTHEW JONATHAN DAWE
AGE 27
BORN: KINGSTON, ON
1 APR 1980 - 4 JUL 2007
3RD BN - PRINCESS PATRICIA'S CANADIAN LIGHT INFANTRY - EDMONTON
2 RCR BG - C COY
KANDAHAR - AFGHANISTAN
VP

ROTO 4 AFGHANISTAN — R4
CPLC CHRISTIAN JCTA DUCHESNE
ÂGE 34
NÉ À MONTRÉAL, QC
24 SEPTEMBRE 1972 AU 22 AOÛT 2007
5E AMBULANCE DE CAMPAGNE VALCARTIER
GROUPEMENT TACTIQUE
3E BATAILLON ROYAL 22E RÉGIMENT
KANDAHAR - AFGHANISTAN

JOINT TASK FORCE AFGHANISTAN — R-3
MCPL ALLAN MAURICE JAMES STEWART
AGE 30
BORN: NEWCASTLE, NEW BRUNSWICK
02 MAY 1976 - 11 APR 2007
THE ROYAL CANADIAN DRAGOONS - PETAWAWA
2 RCR BG, RECCE SQN
KANDAHAR - AFGHANISTAN

JOINT TASK FORCE AFGHANISTAN — R-3
TPR DARRYL JAMES CASWELL
AGE 25
BORN: BOWMANVILLE, ON
31 JUL 1981 - 11 JUNE 2007
THE ROYAL CANADIAN DRAGOONS - PETAWAWA
2 RCR BG, RECCE SQN
KANDAHAR - AFGHANISTAN

TASK FORCE AFGHANISTAN — R-3
CPL JORDAN JAMES ANDERSON
AGE 25
BORN: FROBISHER BAY, NT
21 JUN 1982 - 4 JUL 2007
3RD BN - PRINCESS PATRICIA'S CANADIAN LIGHT INFANTRY - EDMONTON
2 RCR BG - C COY
KANDAHAR - AFGHANISTAN
VP

TASK FORCE AFGHANISTAN — R-3
CAPT JEFFERSON CLIFFORD FRANCIS
AGE 36
BORN: OROMOCTO, NB
11 NOV 1970 - 4 JUL 2007
1 CANADIAN HORSE ARTILLERY - SHILO
2 RCR BG - D BTY
KANDAHAR - AFGHANISTAN

ROTO 4 AFGHANISTAN — R4
ADJUM MARIO JCMM MERCIER
ÂGE 43
NÉ À WEEDON ESTRIE
5 MARS 1964 AU 22 AOÛT 2007
2E BATAILLON ROYAL 22E RÉGIMENT VALCARTIER
GROUPEMENT TACTIQUE
3E BATAILLON ROYAL 22E RÉGIMENT
KANDAHAR - AFGHANISTAN

JOINT TASK FORCE AFGHANISTAN — R-3
MCPL ANTHONY MARK KLUMPENHOUWER
AGE 25
BORN: LISTOWEL, ONTARIO
22 AUG 1981 - 18 APR 2007
CANSOF
KANDAHAR - AFGHANISTAN

TASK FORCE AFGHANISTAN — R-3
CPL STEPHEN FREDERICK BOUZANE
AGE 26
BORN: SPRINGDALE, NL
21 MAR 1981 - 20 JUN 2007
3RD BN - PRINCESS PATRICIA'S CANADIAN LIGHT INFANTRY - EDMONTON
2 RCR BG - C COY
KANDAHAR - AFGHANISTAN
VP

TASK FORCE AFGHANISTAN — R-3
CPL COLE DANIEL BARTSCH
AGE 23
BORN: SASKATOON, SK
01 SEP 1983 - 4 JUL 2007
3RD BN - PRINCESS PATRICIA'S CANADIAN LIGHT INFANTRY - EDMONTON
2 RCR BG - C COY
KANDAHAR - AFGHANISTAN
VP

TASK FORCE AFGHANISTAN — R-3
PTE LANE WILLIAM THOMAS WATKINS
AGE 20
BORN: WINNIPEG, MB
05 DEC 1987 - 4 JUL 2007
3RD BN - PRINCESS PATRICIA'S CANADIAN LIGHT INFANTRY - EDMONTON
2 RCR BG - C COY
KANDAHAR - AFGHANISTAN
VP

AFGHANISTAN
MAJOR RAYMOND MARK RUCKPAUL
AGE 41
BORN: HAMILTON, ON
1 OCTOBER 1965 TO 29 AUGUST 2007
ROYAL CANADIAN DRAGOONS
PETAWAWA, ONTARIO
ISAF HQ
KABUL - AFGHANISTAN
ISAF

CPL NATHAN HORNBURG
AGE 24
BORN CALGARY, AB
19 JUNE 1983 – 24 SEPTEMBER 2007
KING'S OWN CALGARY REGIMENT
GROUPEMENT TACTIQUE
3e BATAILLON ROYAL 22e RÉGIMENT
KANDAHAR - AFGHANISTAN

AFGHANISTAN ROTO 4

CAPORAL ÉRIC EB. LABBÉ
ÂGE 31
NÉ À RIMOUSKI, QUÉBEC
25 JANVIER 1976 AU 6 JANVIER 2008
2e BATAILLON ROYAL 22E RÉGIMENT
GROUPEMENT TACTIQUE 3e BATAILLON
ROYAL 22e RÉGIMENT VALCARTIER
FORCE OPÉRATIONNELLE INTERARMÉES
DE L'AFGHANISTAN 3-07 ROTO 4
KANDAHAR - AFGHANISTAN

AFGHANISTAN ROTO 4

TROOPER MICHAEL YUKI HAYAKAZE
AGE 25
BORN: EDMONTON, AB
9 FEBRUARY 1983 TO 02 MARCH 2008
LORD STRATHCONA'S HORSE (ROYAL CANADIANS),
EDMONTON, ALBERTA
FORCE OPÉRATIONNELLE INTERARMÉES DE
L'AFGHANISTAN 3-07 ROTO 4
KANDAHAR, AFGHANISTAN

AFGHANISTAN ROTO 4

CPL MICHAEL GUNTER STARKER
AGE 36
BORN: CALGARY, AB
16 FEBRUARY 1972 TO 06 MAY 2008
15TH FIELD AMBULANCE
HEALTH SERVICES SUPPORT
INTERNATIONAL SECURITY ASSISTANCE FORCE
TASK FORCE 1-08
KANDAHAR - AFGHANISTAN

AFGHANISTAN ROTO 5

Pte COLIN WILLIAM WILMOT
AGE 24
BORN: FREDERICTON, NB
12 MAY 1984 TO 06 JULY 2008
1 FIELD AMBULANCE
HEALTH SERVICES SUPPORT
INTERNATIONAL SECURITY ASSISTANCE FORCE
TASK FORCE 1-08
KANDAHAR - AFGHANISTAN

AFGHANISTAN ROTO 5

CPL NICOLAS R BEAUCHAMP
ÂGE 28
NÉ À VERDUN, QC
11 JANVIER 1979 AU 17 NOVEMBRE 2007
5e AMB DU C - VALCARTIER
FORCE OPÉRATIONNELLE INTERARMÉES DE
L'AFGHANISTAN 3-07 ROTO 4
3e BATAILLON ROYAL 22E RÉGIMENT
KANDAHAR - AFGHANISTAN

AFGHANISTAN ROTO 4

ADJUDANT HANI MASSOUH
ÂGE 41
NÉ À ALEXANDRIE, ÉGYPTE
9 NOVEMBRE 1966 AU 6 JANVIER 2008
2e BATAILLON ROYAL 22E RÉGIMENT
GROUPEMENT TACTIQUE 3e BATAILLON
ROYAL 22e RÉGIMENT VALCARTIER
FORCE OPÉRATIONNELLE INTERARMÉES
DE L'AFGHANISTAN 3-07 ROTO 4
KANDAHAR - AFGHANISTAN

AFGHANISTAN ROTO 4

BOMBARDIER JÉRÉMIE OUELLET
AGE 22
BORN: MATANE, QC
25 MARCH 1985 TO 11 MARCH 2008
ROYAL CANADIAN HORSE ARTILLERY
SHILO, MANITOBA
INTERNATIONAL SECURITY ASSISTANCE FORCE
TASK FORCE 1-08
KANDAHAR - AFGHANISTAN

AFGHANISTAN ROTO 5

Capt RICHARD STEVEN LEARY
AGE 32
BORN: BRANTFORD, ON
11 SEPTEMBER 1975 TO 03 JUNE 2008
2ND BN - PRINCESS PATRICIA'S CANADIAN LIGHT INFANTRY
2 PPCLI BATTLE GROUP
INTERNATIONAL SECURITY ASSISTANCE FORCE
TASK FORCE 1-08
KANDAHAR - AFGHANISTAN

AFGHANISTAN ROTO 5

Corporal JAMES HAYWARD ARNAL
AGE 25
BORN: KELLINGTON, SK
09 APRIL 1983 TO 19 JULY 2008
2ND BN - PRINCESS PATRICIA'S CANADIAN LIGHT INFANTRY
2 PPCLI BATTLE GROUP
INTERNATIONAL SECURITY ASSISTANCE FORCE
TASK FORCE 1-08
KANDAHAR - AFGHANISTAN

AFGHANISTAN ROTO 5

SOLDAT MICHEL JR. LÉVESQUE
ÂGE 25
NÉ À ST-JEAN-SUR-RICHELIEU, QUÉBEC
15 SEPTEMBRE 1982 AU 17 NOVEMBRE 2007
3e BATAILLON ROYAL 22E RÉGIMENT
GROUPEMENT TACTIQUE 3e BATAILLON
ROYAL 22e RÉGIMENT VALCARTIER
FORCE OPÉRATIONNELLE INTERARMÉES
DE L'AFGHANISTAN 3-07 ROTO 4
KANDAHAR - AFGHANISTAN

AFGHANISTAN ROTO 4

CAVALIER RICHARD RENAUD
ÂGE 26
NÉ À: ALMA, QC
27 NOVEMBRE 1981 AU 15 JANVIER 2008
12E RÉGIMENT BLINDÉ DU CANADA - VALCARTIER
FORCE OPÉRATIONNELLE INTERARMÉES DE
L'AFGHANISTAN 3-07 ROTO 4
3e BATAILLON ROYAL 22e RÉGIMENT
KANDAHAR - AFGHANISTAN

AFGHANISTAN ROTO 4

SERGEANT JASON BOYES
AGE 32
BORN: LYNN LAKE, MB
22 OCTOBER 1975 TO 16 MARCH 2008
2ND BN - PRINCESS PATRICIA'S CANADIAN LIGHT INFANTRY
2 PPCLI BATTLE GROUP
INTERNATIONAL SECURITY ASSISTANCE FORCE
TASK FORCE 1-08
KANDAHAR - AFGHANISTAN

AFGHANISTAN ROTO 5

Captain JONATHAN SUTHERLAND SNYDER
AGE 26
BORN: PENTICTON, BC
20 DECEMBER 1981 TO 07 JUNE 2008
1ST BN - PRINCESS PATRICIA'S CANADIAN LIGHT INFANTRY
OPERATIONAL MENTORING AND LIAISON TEAM
INTERNATIONAL SECURITY ASSISTANCE FORCE
TASK FORCE 1-08
KANDAHAR - AFGHANISTAN

AFGHANISTAN ROTO 5

Master Corporal JOSHUA BRIAN ROBERTS
AGE 29
BORN: SASKATOON, SK
08 SEPTEMBER 1978 TO 09 AUGUST 2008
2ND BN - PRINCESS PATRICIA'S CANADIAN LIGHT INFANTRY
2 PPCLI BATTLE GROUP
INTERNATIONAL SECURITY ASSISTANCE FORCE
TASK FORCE 1-08
KANDAHAR - AFGHANISTAN

AFGHANISTAN ROTO 5

ARTILLEUR JONATHAN JJJ DION
ÂGE 27
NÉ À: VAL-D'OR, QC
10 JANVIER 1980 AU 30 DÉCEMBRE 2007
5E RÉGIMENT D'ARTILLERIE LÉGÈRE
DU CANADA-VALCARTIER
FORCE OPÉRATIONNELLE INTERARMÉES
DE L'AFGHANISTAN 3-07 ROTO 4
3e BATAILLON ROYAL 22e RÉGIMENT
KANDAHAR - AFGHANISTAN

AFGHANISTAN ROTO 4

SAP ÉTIENNE JFE GONTHIER
ÂGE 21
NÉ À: QUÉBEC, QC
3 FÉVRIER 1986 AU 23 JANVIER 2008
5e RÉGIMENT GÉNIE DU CANADA - VALCARTIER
FORCE OPÉRATIONNELLE INTERARMÉES DE
L'AFGHANISTAN 3-07 ROTO 4
3e BATAILLON ROYAL 22e RÉGIMENT
KANDAHAR - AFGHANISTAN

AFGHANISTAN ROTO 4

Pte TERRY JOHN STREET
AGE 24
BORN: HULL, QC
24 AUGUST 1983 – 4 APRIL 2008
2ND BN - PRINCESS PATRICIA'S CANADIAN LIGHT INFANTRY
2 PPCLI BATTLE GROUP
INTERNATIONAL SECURITY ASSISTANCE FORCE
TASK FORCE 1-08
KANDAHAR - AFGHANISTAN

AFGHANISTAN ROTO 5

Corporal BRENDAN DOWNEY
AGE 36
BORN: MONTREAL, QC
26 JUNE 1972 TO 04 JUNE 2008
MILITARY POLICE, CFB WAINWPEG DET DUNDURN
THEATRE INTERARMÉES ELEMENT
INTERNATIONAL SECURITY ASSISTANCE FORCE
TASK FORCE 1-08
CAMP MIRAGE

AFGHANISTAN ROTO 5

Master Corporal ERIN MELVIN DOYLE
AGE 32
BORN: MAPLE RIDGE, BC
20 JUNE 1976 TO 11 AUGUST 2008
2ND BN - PRINCESS PATRICIA'S CANADIAN LIGHT INFANTRY
2 PPCLI BATTLE GROUP
INTERNATIONAL SECURITY ASSISTANCE FORCE
TASK FORCE 1-08
KANDAHAR - AFGHANISTAN

AFGHANISTAN ROTO 5

AFGHANISTAN · ROTO 5

SERGEANT SHAWN ALLEN EADES
AGE 33
BORN: HAMILTON, ON
26 MARCH 1975 TO 20 AUGUST 2008
1 COMBAT ENGINEER REGIMENT
2 PPCLI BATTLE GROUP
INTERNATIONAL SECURITY ASSISTANCE FORCE
TASK FORCE 1-08
KANDAHAR - AFGHANISTAN

PRIVATE CHADWICK JAMES HORN
AGE 21
BORN: CALGARY, AB
14 OCTOBER 1986 TO 03 SEPTEMBER 2008
2ND BN - PRINCESS PATRICIA'S CANADIAN LIGHT INFANTRY
2 PPCLI BATTLE GROUP
INTERNATIONAL SECURITY ASSISTANCE FORCE
TASK FORCE 1-08
KANDAHAR - AFGHANISTAN

CORPORAL MARK ROBERT McLAREN
AGE: 23
BORN: TORONTO, ONTARIO
07 SEPTEMBER, 1985 TO 05 DECEMBER, 2008
1ST BATTALION - THE ROYAL CANADIAN REGIMENT
OPERATIONAL MENTOR AND LIAISON TEAM
INTERNATIONAL SECURITY ASSISTANCE FORCE
TASK FORCE 3-08 ROTO 6
KANDAHAR - AFGHANISTAN

PRIVATE JUSTIN PETER JONES
AGE: 21
BORN: GRAND FALLS, NEWFOUNDLAND & LABRADOR
24 NOVEMBER 1987 TO 13 DECEMBER 2008
2ND BATTALION - THE ROYAL CANADIAN REGIMENT
KANDAHAR PROVINCIAL RECONSTRUCTION TEAM
INTERNATIONAL SECURITY ASSISTANCE FORCE
TASK FORCE 3-08 ROTO 6
KANDAHAR - AFGHANISTAN

TROOPER BRIAN RICHARD GOOD
AGE: 43
BORN: ZWEIBRÜCKEN, GERMANY
16 JANUARY 1965 TO 07 JANUARY 2009
ROYAL CANADIAN DRAGOONS
3 RCR BATTLE GROUP
INTERNATIONAL SECURITY ASSISTANCE FORCE
TASK FORCE 3-08 ROTO 6
KANDAHAR - AFGHANISTAN

SAPPER STEPHAN JOHN STOCK
AGE 25
BORN: CAMPBELL RIVER, BC
03 JUNE 1983 TO 20 AUGUST 2008
1 COMBAT ENGINEER REGIMENT
2 PPCLI BATTLE GROUP
INTERNATIONAL SECURITY ASSISTANCE FORCE
TASK FORCE 1-08
KANDAHAR - AFGHANISTAN

CPL MICHAEL JAMES ALEXANDER SEGGIE
AGE 21
BORN: CALGARY, AB
22 NOVEMBER 1986 TO 03 SEPTEMBER 2008
2ND BN - PRINCESS PATRICIA'S CANADIAN LIGHT INFANTRY
2 PPCLI BATTLE GROUP
INTERNATIONAL SECURITY ASSISTANCE FORCE
TASK FORCE 1-08
KANDAHAR - AFGHANISTAN

WARRANT OFFICER ROBERT JOHN WILSON
AGE: 37
BORN: NEWMARKET, ONTARIO
16 APRIL 1971 TO 05 DECEMBER 2008
1ST BATTALION - THE ROYAL CANADIAN REGIMENT
OPERATIONAL MENTOR AND LIAISON TEAM
INTERNATIONAL SECURITY ASSISTANCE FORCE
TASK FORCE 3-08 ROTO 6
KANDAHAR - AFGHANISTAN

PRIVATE MICHAEL BRUCE FREEMAN
AGE: 28
BORN: PETERBOROUGH, ONTARIO
03 DECEMBER 1980 TO 26 DECEMBER 2008
3RD BATTALION - THE ROYAL CANADIAN REGIMENT
3 RCR BATTLE GROUP
INTERNATIONAL SECURITY ASSISTANCE FORCE
TASK FORCE 3-08 ROTO 6
KANDAHAR - AFGHANISTAN

SAPPER SEAN DAVID GREENFIELD
AGE 25
BORN: PINAWA, MANITOBA
10 MARCH 1983 TO 31 JANUARY 2009
2 COMBAT ENGINEER REGIMENT
3 RCR BATTLE GROUP
INTERNATIONAL SECURITY ASSISTANCE FORCE
TASK FORCE 3-08 ROTO 6
KANDAHAR - AFGHANISTAN

CORPORAL DUSTIN ROY ROBERT JOSEPH WASDEN
AGE 25
BORN: PRINCE ALBERT, SK
24 JULY 1983 TO 20 AUGUST 2008
1 COMBAT ENGINEER REGIMENT
2 PPCLI BATTLE GROUP
INTERNATIONAL SECURITY ASSISTANCE FORCE
TASK FORCE 1-08
KANDAHAR - AFGHANISTAN

SERGEANT PRESCOTT SHIPWAY
AGE 36
BORN: HARLOW ESSEX, UNITED KINGDOM
13 JANUARY 1972 TO 07 SEPTEMBER 2008
2ND BN - PRINCESS PATRICIA'S CANADIAN LIGHT INFANTRY
2 PPCLI BATTLE GROUP
INTERNATIONAL SECURITY ASSISTANCE FORCE
TASK FORCE 1-08
KANDAHAR - AFGHANISTAN

PRIVATE JOHN MICHAEL ROY CURWIN
AGE 26
BORN: HALIFAX, NOVA SCOTIA
01 MARCH 1982 TO 13 DECEMBER 2008
2ND BATTALION - THE ROYAL CANADIAN REGIMENT
KANDAHAR PROVINCIAL RECONSTRUCTION TEAM
INTERNATIONAL SECURITY ASSISTANCE FORCE
TASK FORCE 3-08 ROTO 6
KANDAHAR - AFGHANISTAN

SERGEANT GREGORY JOHN KRUSE
AGE 40
BORN: CAMPBELLTON, NEW BRUNSWICK
02 DECEMBER 1968 TO 27 DECEMBER 2008
2 COMBAT ENGINEER REGIMENT
3 RCR BATTLE GROUP
INTERNATIONAL SECURITY ASSISTANCE FORCE
TASK FORCE 3-08 ROTO 6
KANDAHAR - AFGHANISTAN

WARRANT OFFICER DENNIS RAYMOND BROWN
AGE 38
BORN: ST.CATHARINES ONTARIO
26 AUGUST 1970 TO 03 MARCH 2009
THE LINCOLN AND WELLAND REGIMENT
JTF AFGHANISTAN NCE COUNTER-IED
INTERNATIONAL SECURITY ASSISTANCE FORCE
TASK FORCE 3-08 ROTO 6
KANDAHAR - AFGHANISTAN

CORPORAL ANDREW PAUL GRENON
AGE 23
BORN: WINDSOR, ON
19 JANUARY 1985 TO 03 SEPTEMBER 2008
2ND BN - PRINCESS PATRICIA'S CANADIAN LIGHT INFANTRY
2 PPCLI BATTLE GROUP
INTERNATIONAL SECURITY ASSISTANCE FORCE
TASK FORCE 1-08
KANDAHAR - AFGHANISTAN

PRIVATE DEMETRIOS DIPLAROS
AGE: 24
BORN: EAST YORK, ONTARIO
21 NOVEMBER 1984 TO 05 DECEMBER 2008
1ST BATTALION - THE ROYAL CANADIAN REGIMENT
OPERATIONAL MENTOR AND LIAISON TEAM
INTERNATIONAL SECURITY ASSISTANCE FORCE
TASK FORCE 3-08 ROTO 6
KANDAHAR - AFGHANISTAN

CORPORAL THOMAS JAMES HAMILTON
AGE: 26
BORN: TRURO, NOVA SCOTIA
18 APRIL 1982 TO 13 DECEMBER 2008
2ND BATTALION - THE ROYAL CANADIAN REGIMENT
KANDAHAR PROVINCIAL RECONSTRUCTION TEAM
INTERNATIONAL SECURITY ASSISTANCE FORCE
TASK FORCE 3-08 ROTO 6
KANDAHAR - AFGHANISTAN

ADJUDANT GAÉTAN JMJF ROBERGE
AGE: 45
NÉ À SACRÉ-COEUR, QUÉBEC
14 JANVIER 1963 AU 27 DÉCEMBRE 2008
2ND BATTALION IRISH REGIMENT OF CANADA
OPERATIONAL MENTOR AND LIAISON TEAM
INTERNATIONAL SECURITY ASSISTANCE FORCE
TASK FORCE 3-08 ROTO 6
KANDAHAR - AFGHANISTAN

CAPORAL DANY OLIVIER FORTIN
ÂGE: 29
NÉ À BAIE COMEAU, QUÉBEC
05 OCTOBRE 1979 AU 03 MARS 2009
42E ESCADRON TACTIQUE
JTF AFGHANISTAN NCE COUNTER-IED
INTERNATIONAL SECURITY ASSISTANCE FORCE
TASK FORCE 3-08 ROTO 6
KANDAHAR - AFGHANISTAN

AFGHANISTAN

CORPORAL KENNETH CHAD O'QUINN
AGE: 25
Born: GOOSE BAY NEWFOUNDLAND
25 JANUARY 1984 TO 03 MARCH 2009
2 CMBG HQ & SIGS SQN
JTF AFGHANISTAN NCE COUNTER IED
INTERNATIONAL SECURITY ASSISTANCE FORCE
TASK FORCE 3-08 ROTO 6
KANDAHAR - AFGHANISTAN

AFGHANISTAN

TROOPER COREY JOSEPH HAYES
AGE: 22
BORN: BELLEVILLE, ONTARIO
02 JANUARY 1987 TO 20 MARCH 2009
ROYAL CANADIAN DRAGOONS
3 RCR BATTLE GROUP
INTERNATIONAL SECURITY ASSISTANCE FORCE
TASK FORCE 3-08 ROTO 6
KANDAHAR - AFGHANISTAN

AFGHANISTAN

SOLDAT ALEXANDRE AJ PÉLOQUIN
ÂGE: 21
NÉ À SAINT-JÉRÔME, QUÉBEC
27 DÉCEMBRE 1988 AU 08 JUIN 2009
FORCE OPÉRATIONNELLE INTERARMÉES
DE L'AFGHANISTAN 1-09 ROTO 7
GROUPEMENT TACTIQUE 2e BATAILLON
ROYAL 22e RÉGIMENT VALCARTIER

AFGHANISTAN

CAPORAL-CHEF PATRICE AUDET
ÂGE: 38
NÉ À MONTRÉAL, QUÉBEC
19 AVRIL 1971 AU 6 JUILLET 2009
430e ESCADRON TACTIQUE D'HÉLICOPTÈRES
FORCE CANADIENNE D'HÉLICOPTÈRES AFGHANISTAN
FORCE OPÉRATIONNELLE INTERARMÉES
DE L'AFGHANISTAN 1-09 ROTO 7
KANDAHAR - AFGHANISTAN

AFGHANISTAN

CAPORAL CHRISTIAN C. BOBBITT
ÂGE: 23
NÉ À SEPT-ÎLES, QUÉBEC
12 SEPTEMBRE 1985 AU 1 AOÛT 2009
5e RÉGIMENT DE GÉNIE DE COMBAT
GROUPEMENT TACTIQUE 2e BATAILLON
ROYAL 22e RÉGIMENT VALCARTIER

AFGHANISTAN

TROOPER MARC DIAB
AGE: 22
BORN: AJREBEL, LEBANON
23 SEPTEMBRE 1986 TO 08 MARCH 2009
ROYAL CANADIAN DRAGOONS
3 RCR BATTLE GROUP
INTERNATIONAL SECURITY ASSISTANCE FORCE
TASK FORCE 3-08 ROTO 6
KANDAHAR - AFGHANISTAN

AFGHANISTAN

MASTER CORPORAL SCOTT FRANCIS VERNELLI
AGE: 28
BORN: SAULT STE MARIE, ONTARIO
06 MAY 1980 TO 20 MARCH 2009
3RD BATTALION - THE ROYAL CANADIAN REGIMENT
3 RCR BATTLE GROUP
INTERNATIONAL SECURITY ASSISTANCE FORCE
TASK FORCE 3-08 ROTO 6
KANDAHAR - AFGHANISTAN

AFGHANISTAN

CAPORAL MARTIN JRM DUBÉ
ÂGE: 35
NÉ À QUÉBEC, QUÉBEC
27 JUIN 1973 AU 14 JUIN 2009
5e RÉGIMENT DE GÉNIE DE COMBAT
53e ESCADRON C-IED CENTRE DE COORDINATION
D'APPUI DU GÉNIE DE LA FOI AFG
FORCE OPÉRATIONNELLE INTERARMÉES
DE L'AFGHANISTAN 1-09 ROTO 7
KANDAHAR - AFGHANISTAN

AFGHANISTAN

CAPORAL MARTIN JOANNETTE
ÂGE: 25
NÉ À ST-CALIXTE, QUÉBEC
2 SEPTEMBRE 1983 AU 6 JUILLET 2009
2e BATAILLON ROYAL 22e RÉGIMENT
FORCE CANADIENNE D'HÉLICOPTÈRES AFGHANISTAN
FORCE OPÉRATIONNELLE INTERARMÉES
DE L'AFGHANISTAN 1-09 ROTO 7
KANDAHAR - AFGHANISTAN

AFGHANISTAN

CAPORAL JEAN- FRANCOIS J. DROUIN
ÂGE: 31
NÉ À QUÉBEC, QUÉBEC
30 MAI 1978 AU 6 SEPTEMBRE 2009
5e RÉGIMENT DE GÉNIE DE COMBAT
GROUPEMENT TACTIQUE 2e BATAILLON
ROYAL 22e RÉGIMENT VALCARTIER

AFGHANISTAN

TROOPER JACK BOUTHILLIER
AGE: 20
BORN: HEARST, ONTARIO
13 SEPTEMBER 1988 TO 20 MARCH 2009
ROYAL CANADIAN DRAGOONS
3 RCR BATTLE GROUP
INTERNATIONAL SECURITY ASSISTANCE FORCE
TASK FORCE 3-08 ROTO 6
KANDAHAR - AFGHANISTAN

AFGHANISTAN

CAVALIER KARINE MN BLAIS
AGE: 21
NÉ À COWANSVILLE, QUÉBEC
04 JANVIER 1988 AU 13 AVRIL 2009
12e RÉGIMENT BLINDÉ DU CANADA
GROUPEMENT TACTIQUE 2e BATAILLON
ROYAL 22e RÉGIMENT - VALCARTIER

AFGHANISTAN

CORPORAL NICK ASHLEY BULGER
AGE: 30
BORN: TORONTO, ONTARIO
4 JUNE 1979 TO 2 JULY 2009
3RD BN - PRINCESS PATRICIA'S CANADIAN LIGHT INFANTRY
JOINT TASK FORCE AFGHANISTAN HQ
KANDAHAR - AFGHANISTAN

AFGHANISTAN

SOLDAT SÉBASTIEN COURCY
ÂGE: 26
NÉ À ST-HYACINTHE, QUÉBEC
14 MARS 1983 AU 16 JUILLET 2009
2e BATAILLON ROYAL 22e RÉGIMENT
GROUPEMENT TACTIQUE 2e BATAILLON
ROYAL 22e RÉGIMENT - VALCARTIER
FORCE OPÉRATIONNELLE INTERARMÉES
DE L'AFGHANISTAN 1-09 ROTO 7
KANDAHAR - AFGHANISTAN

AFGHANISTAN

MAJOR YANNICK JYFS. PEPIN
ÂGE: 36
NÉ À ARTHABASKA, QUÉBEC
8 SEPTEMBRE 1973 AU 6 SEPTEMBRE 2009
5e RÉGIMENT DE GÉNIE DE COMBAT
GROUPEMENT TACTIQUE 2e BATAILLON
ROYAL 22e RÉGIMENT VALCARTIER

AFGHANISTAN

CORPORAL TYLER CROOKS
AGE: 24
BORN: WELLAND, ONTARIO
20 MARCH 1985 TO 20 MARCH 2009
3RD BATTALION - THE ROYAL CANADIAN REGIMENT
3 RCR BATTLE GROUP
INTERNATIONAL SECURITY ASSISTANCE FORCE
TASK FORCE I-08 ROTO 6
KANDAHAR - AFGHANISTAN

AFGHANISTAN

MAJOR MICHELLE MENDES
AGE: 30
BORN: COBOURG, ONTARIO
21 JULY 1978 TO 04 APRIL 2009
CHIEF OF DEFENCE INTELLIGENCE
KANDAHAR INTELLIGENCE FUSION CENTRE
INTERNATIONAL SECURITY ASSISTANCE FORCE
TASK FORCE 1-09 ROTO 7
KANDAHAR - AFGHANISTAN

AFGHANISTAN

CAPORAL CHEF CHARLES-PHILIPPE MICHAUD
ÂGE: 28
NÉ À BATHURST, NOUVEAU-BRUNSWICK
29 MARS 1981 AU 04 JUILLET 2009
2e BATAILLON ROYAL 22e RÉGIMENT
GROUPEMENT TACTIQUE 2e BATAILLON ROYAL 22e RÉGIMENT
VALCARTIER
FORCE OPÉRATIONNELLE INTERARMÉES
DE L'AFGHANISTAN 1-09 ROTO 7
KANDAHAR - AFGHANISTAN

AFGHANISTAN

SAPEUR MATTHIEU JPGM. ALLARD
ÂGE: 20
NÉ À VAL-D'OR, QUÉBEC
4 SEPTEMBRE 1988 AU 13 AOÛT 2009
5e RÉGIMENT DE GÉNIE DE COMBAT
GROUPEMENT TACTIQUE 2e BATAILLON
ROYAL 22e RÉGIMENT VALCARTIER

AFGHANISTAN

SOLDAT PATRICK PJ . LORMAND
ÂGE: 21
NÉ À HAWKESBURY, ONTARIO
11 FÉVRIER 1988 AU 13 SEPTEMBRE 2009
2e BATAILLON ROYAL 22e RÉGIMENT
GROUPEMENT TACTIQUE 2e BATAILLON
ROYAL 22e RÉGIMENT VALCARTIER
FORCE OPÉRATIONNELLE INTERARMÉES
DE L'AFGHANISTAN 1-09 ROTO 7
KANDAHAR - AFGHANISTAN

AFGHANISTAN

SOLDAT JONATHAN JSJ. COUTURIER
AGE: 23
NÉ À LORETTEVILLE, QUÉBEC
2 AVRIL 1986 AU 17 SEPTEMBRE 2009
2E BATAILLON ROYAL 22E RÉGIMENT
GROUPEMENT TACTIQUE 2E BATAILLON
ROYAL 22E RÉGIMENT VALCARTIER

FORCE OPÉRATIONNELLE INTERARMÉES
DE L'AFGHANISTAN 1-09 ROTO 7
KANDAHAR - AFGHANISTAN

AFGHANISTAN

PRIVATE GARRETT WILLIAM CHIDLEY
AGE: 21
BORN CAMBRIDGE, ONTARIO
22 MARCH 1988 TO 30 DECEMBER 2009
2ND BN PRINCESS PATRICIA'S CANADIAN LIGHT INFANTRY
KANDAHAR PROVINCIAL RECONSTRUCTION TEAM STAB A

INTERNATIONAL SECURITY ASSISTANCE FORCE
TASK FORCE 3-09 ROTO 8
KANDAHAR - AFGHANISTAN

AFGHANISTAN

SERGEANT JOHN WAYNE FAUGHT
AGE: 44
BORN SAULT STE MARIE, ONTARIO
20 APRIL 1965 TO 16 JANUARY 2010
1ST BATTALION PRINCESS PATRICIA'S CANADIAN LIGHT INFANTRY
DELTA COMPANY (PPCLI) BATTLE GROUP

INTERNATIONAL SECURITY ASSISTANCE FORCE
TASK FORCE 3-09 ROTO 8
KANDAHAR - AFGHANISTAN

AFGHANISTAN

PRIVATE TYLER WILLIAM TODD
AGE: 26
BORN KITCHENER, ONTARIO
13 JULY 1983 TO 11 APRIL 2010
1ST BATTALION PRINCESS PATRICIA'S CANADIAN LIGHT INFANTRY
DELTA COMPANY (PPCLI) BATTLE GROUP

INTERNATIONAL SECURITY ASSISTANCE FORCE
TASK FORCE 3-09 ROTO 8
KANDAHAR - AFGHANISTAN

AFGHANISTAN

TROOPER LARRY JOHN ZUIDEMA RUDD
AGE: 26
BRANTFORD, ONTARIO
21 AUGUST 1983 TO 24 MAY 2010
ROYAL CANADIAN DRAGOONS - PETAWAWA
RECCE SQUADRON, 1 RCR BG

INTERNATIONAL SECURITY ASSISTANCE FORCE
TASK FORCE 1-10 ROTO 9
KANDAHAR - AFGHANISTAN

AFGHANISTAN

ROTO 5

SERGEANT JASON BOYES
AGE 32
BORN LYNN LAKE, MB
22 OCTOBER 1975 TO 16 MARCH 2008
2ND BN PRINCESS PATRICIA'S CANADIAN LIGHT INFANTRY
2 PPCLI BATTLE GROUP

INTERNATIONAL SECURITY ASSISTANCE FORCE
TASK FORCE 1-08
KANDAHAR - AFGHANISTAN

AFGHANISTAN

MICHELLE LANG
AGE: 34
BORN VANCOUVER, BRITISH COLUMBIA
31 JANUARY 1975 TO 30 DECEMBER 2009
THE CALGARY HERALD CANWEST GLOBAL
EMBEDDED JOURNALIST

INTERNATIONAL SECURITY ASSISTANCE FORCE
TASK FORCE 3-09
KANDAHAR - AFGHANISTAN

AFGHANISTAN

CAPTAIN CECIL FRANCIS, (FRANK) PAUL
AGE: 53
BORN BADGER, NEWFOUNDLAND
02 JULY 1956 TO 10 FEBRUARY 2010
28 FIELD AMBULANCE, OTTAWA

HEALTH SERVICES UNIT: JTF AFGHANISTAN
TASK FORCE 3-09
KANDAHAR - AFGHANISTAN

AFGHANISTAN

PO2 DOUGLAS CRAIG BLAKE
AGE: 37
BORN SIMCOE, ONTARIO
21 MAY 1972 TO 03 MAY 2010
FLEET DIVING UNIT - ATLANTIC
C-IED SQUADRON - JTF AFGHANISTAN

INTERNATIONAL SECURITY ASSISTANCE FORCE
TASK FORCE 1-10 ROTO 9
KANDAHAR - AFGHANISTAN

AFGHANISTAN

BOMBARDIER KARL MANNING
AGE: 31 ANS
NÉ À CHICOUTIMI, QUÉBEC
03 FÉVRIER 1980 AU 27 MAI 2011
5E RÉGIMENT D'ARTILLERIE LÉGÈRE DU CANADA
GROUPEMENT TACTIQUE DU 1ER BATAILLON
ROYAL 22E RÉGIMENT VALCARTIER

FORCE OPÉRATIONNELLE INTERARMÉES
DE L'AFGHANISTAN 3-10 ROTO 10
KANDAHAR, AFGHANISTAN

AFGHANISTAN

SAPPER STEVEN HENRY MARSHALL
AGE: 24
BORN CALGARY, ALBERTA
12 JANUARY 1985 TO 30 DECEMBER 2009
1 FIELD ENGINEER REGIMENT
11 FIELD SQUADRON, 1 PPCLI BATTLE GROUP

INTERNATIONAL SECURITY ASSISTANCE FORCE
TASK FORCE 3-09 ROTO 8
KANDAHAR - AFGHANISTAN

AFGHANISTAN

CORPORAL ZACHERY WILFRID McCORMACK
AGE: 21
BORN EDMONTON, ALBERTA
14 MARCH 1988 TO 30 DECEMBER 2009
THE LOYAL EDMONTON REGIMENT
KANDAHAR PROVINCIAL RECONSTRUCTION TEAM STAB A

INTERNATIONAL SECURITY ASSISTANCE FORCE
TASK FORCE 3-09 ROTO 8
KANDAHAR - AFGHANISTAN

AFGHANISTAN

CORPORAL JOSHUA CALEB BAKER
AGE: 24
BORN SCARBOROUGH, ONTARIO
14 JUNE 1985 TO 12 FEBRUARY 2010
THE LOYAL EDMONTON REGIMENT
KANDAHAR PROVINCIAL RECONSTRUCTION TEAM STAB A

INTERNATIONAL SECURITY ASSISTANCE FORCE
TASK FORCE 3-09 ROTO 8
KANDAHAR - AFGHANISTAN

AFGHANISTAN

PRIVATE KEVIN THOMAS McKAY
AGE: 24
BORN RICHMOND HILL, ONTARIO
28 FEBRUARY 1986 TO 13 MAY 2010
1ST BN PRINCESS PATRICIA'S CANADIAN LIGHT INFANTRY
DELTA COMPANY / PPCLI BATTLE GROUP

INTERNATIONAL SECURITY ASSISTANCE FORCE
TASK FORCE 3-09 ROTO 8
KANDAHAR - AFGHANISTAN

AFGHANISTAN

SERGEANT MARTIN RENE GOUDREAULT
AGE: 35
BORN SUDBURY, ONTARIO
19 NOVEMBER 1974 TO 06 JUNE 2010
1 COMBAT ENGINEER REGIMENT
1 RCR BG

INTERNATIONAL SECURITY ASSISTANCE FORCE
TASK FORCE 1-10 ROTO 9
KANDAHAR - AFGHANISTAN

AFGHANISTAN

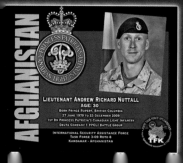

LIEUTENANT ANDREW RICHARD NUTTALL
AGE: 30
BORN PRINCE RUPERT, BRITISH COLUMBIA
27 JUNE 1979 TO 23 DECEMBER 2009
1ST BN PRINCESS PATRICIA'S CANADIAN LIGHT INFANTRY
DELTA COMPANY / PPCLI BATTLE GROUP

INTERNATIONAL SECURITY ASSISTANCE FORCE
TASK FORCE 3-09 ROTO 8
KANDAHAR - AFGHANISTAN

AFGHANISTAN

SERGEANT KIRK GARRET TAYLOR
AGE: 28
BORN YARMOUTH, NOVA SCOTIA
10 APRIL 1981 TO 30 DECEMBER 2009
2ND FIELD BATTERY
KANDAHAR PROVINCIAL RECONSTRUCTION TEAM STAB A

INTERNATIONAL SECURITY ASSISTANCE FORCE
TASK FORCE 3-09 ROTO 8
KANDAHAR - AFGHANISTAN

AFGHANISTAN

CORPORAL DARREN JAMES FITZPATRICK
AGE: 21
BORN BURNABY, BRITISH COLUMBIA
1 JUNE 1988 TO 20 MARCH 2010
3RD BN PRINCESS PATRICIA'S CANADIAN LIGHT INFANTRY
OPERATIONAL MENTOR AND LIAISON TEAM

INTERNATIONAL SECURITY ASSISTANCE FORCE
TASK FORCE 3-09 ROTO 8
KANDAHAR - AFGHANISTAN

AFGHANISTAN

COLONEL GEOFFREY STEPHEN PARKER
AGE: 42
BORN OAKVILLE, ONTARIO
18 JANUARY 1968 TO 18 MAY 2010
JTF AFGHANISTAN

INTERNATIONAL SECURITY ASSISTANCE FORCE
REGIONAL COMMAND SOUTH
KABUL - AFGHANISTAN

AFGHANISTAN

SERGEANT JAMES PATRICK MacNEIL
AGE: 28
BORN GLACE BAY, NOVA SCOTIA
17 JULY 1981 TO 21 JUNE 2010
2 COMBAT ENGINEER REGIMENT
1 RCR BG

INTERNATIONAL SECURITY ASSISTANCE FORCE
TASK FORCE 1-10 ROTO 9
KANDAHAR - AFGHANISTAN

AFGHANISTAN

Master Corporal Kristal Lee-Anne Giesebrecht
AGE: 34
BORN: WALLACEBURG, ONTARIO
02 OCTOBER 1975 TO 26 JUNE 2010
1 CANADIAN FIELD HOSPITAL
HEALTH SERVICES UNIT

INTERNATIONAL SECURITY ASSISTANCE FORCE
TASK FORCE 1-10 ROTO 9
KANDAHAR - AFGHANISTAN

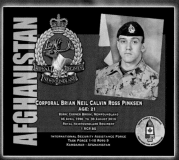

AFGHANISTAN

Corporal Brian Neil Calvin Ross Pinksen
AGE: 21
BORN: CORNER BROOK, NEWFOUNDLAND
08 APRIL 1990 TO 30 AUGUST 2010
ROYAL NEWFOUNDLAND REGIMENT
1 RCR BG

INTERNATIONAL SECURITY ASSISTANCE FORCE
TASK FORCE 1-10 ROTO 9
KANDAHAR - AFGHANISTAN

AFGHANISTAN

Master Corporal Byron Garth Greff
AGE: 28
BORN: SWIFT CURRENT, SASKATCHEWAN
11 AUGUST 1983 TO 29 OCTOBER 2011
3RD BATTALION PRINCESS PATRICIA'S CANADIAN LIGHT INFANTRY

INTERNATIONAL SECURITY ASSISTANCE FORCE
CCTM-A, OP ATTENTION ROTO 0
KABUL - AFGHANISTAN

AFGHANISTAN

CPL KEITH ERIC ESSARY
AGE: 20
24 MARCH 1988 - 08 JANUARY 2009
BORN: DYERSBURG, TN
2D BATTALION, 2D INFANTRY REGIMENT
3RD BRIGADE, 1ST INFANTRY DIVISION
RAMROD

INTERNATIONAL SECURITY ASSISTANCE FORCE
TASK FORCE RAMROD
KANDAHAR - AFGHANISTAN

OEF IX

AFGHANISTAN

CPL JONATHAN MICHAEL WALLS
AGE: 27
BORN IN WEST LAWN, PA
07 FEBRUARY 1982 TO 01 AUGUST 2009
1ST BATTALION, 12TH INFANTRY REGIMENT
HEADQUARTERS PLATOON, CHARLIE COMPANY

INTERNATIONAL SECURITY ASSISTANCE FORCE
TF 1-12 IN
KANDAHAR - AFGHANISTAN

AFGHANISTAN

Private Andrew Christopher Alexander Miller
AGE: 21
BORN: SUDBURY, ONTARIO
31 DECEMBER 1988 TO 26 JUNE 2010
2 FIELD AMBULANCE
HEALTH SERVICES UNIT

INTERNATIONAL SECURITY ASSISTANCE FORCE
TASK FORCE 1-10 ROTO 9
KANDAHAR - AFGHANISTAN

AFGHANISTAN

Caporal Steve J.L. Martin
AGE: 24
NÉ À DRUMMONDVILLE, QUÉBEC
20 DÉCEMBRE 1985 AU 19 DÉCEMBRE 2010
1ER BATAILLON ROYAL 22E RÉGIMENT
GROUPEMENT TACTIQUE DU 1ER BATAILLON
ROYAL 22E RÉGIMENT VALCARTIER

FORCE OPÉRATIONNELLE INTERARMÉES
DE L'AFGHANISTAN 3-10 ROTO 10
KANDAHAR, AFGHANISTAN

US SERVICEMEN AND WOMEN UNDER CANADIAN COMMAND

AFGHANISTAN

SSG JOSHUA LEE RATH
AGE: 22
17 JANUARY 1986 - 08 JANUARY 2009
BORN: DECATUR, AL
2D BATTALION, 2D INFANTRY REGIMENT
3RD BRIGADE, 1ST INFANTRY DIVISION
RAMROD

INTERNATIONAL SECURITY ASSISTANCE FORCE
TASK FORCE RAMROD

OEF IX

AFGHANISTAN

CPL JONATHAN MICHAEL WALLS
AGE: 27
BORN IN WEST LAWN, PA
07 FEBRUARY 1982 TO 01 AUGUST 2009
1ST BATTALION, 12TH INFANTRY REGIMENT
HEADQUARTERS PLATOON, CHARLIE COMPANY

INTERNATIONAL SECURITY ASSISTANCE FORCE
TF 1-12 IN
KANDAHAR - AFGHANISTAN

AFGHANISTAN

Sapper Brian James Collier
AGE: 24
BORN: TORONTO, ONTARIO
06 JULY 1986 TO 20 JULY 2010
1 COMBAT ENGINEER REGIMENT
1 RCR BG

INTERNATIONAL SECURITY ASSISTANCE FORCE
TASK FORCE 1-10 ROTO 9
KANDAHAR - AFGHANISTAN

AFGHANISTAN

Caporal Yannick M.A.Y Scherrer
AGE: 24
NÉ À MONTRÉAL, QUÉBEC
20 JUIN 1986 AU 27 MARS 2011
1ER BATAILLON ROYAL 22E RÉGIMENT
GROUPEMENT TACTIQUE DU 1ER BATAILLON
ROYAL 22E RÉGIMENT VALCARTIER

FORCE OPÉRATIONNELLE INTERARMÉES
DE L'AFGHANISTAN 3-10 ROTO 10
KANDAHAR, AFGHANISTAN

AFGHANISTAN

Paula Loyd
AGE: 36
BORN: SAN ANTONIO, TEXAS
9 JUNE 1972 TO 7 JANUARY 2009
HUMAN TERRAIN SYSTEM
SOCIAL SCIENTIST

INTERNATIONAL SECURITY ASSISTANCE FORCE
COMBINED JOINT TASK FORCE - 76
KANDAHAR - AFGHANISTAN

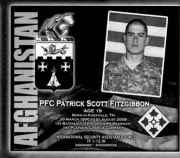

AFGHANISTAN

PFC PATRICK SCOTT FITZGIBBON
AGE: 19
BORN IN KNOXVILLE, TN
30 MARCH 1990 TO 01 AUGUST 2009
1ST BATTALION, 12TH INFANTRY REGIMENT
1ST PLATOON, CHARLIE COMPANY

INTERNATIONAL SECURITY ASSISTANCE FORCE
TF 1-12 IN
KANDAHAR - AFGHANISTAN

AFGHANISTAN

PFC DEVIN JAY MICHEL
AGE: 19
BORN IN ALVIN, IL
03 AUGUST 1990 TO 24 OCTOBER 2009
1ST BATTALION, 12TH INFANTRY REGIMENT
3RD PLATOON, CHARLIE COMPANY

INTERNATIONAL SECURITY ASSISTANCE FORCE
TF 1-12 IN
KANDAHAR - AFGHANISTAN

AFGHANISTAN

Marc J.B. Cyr
AGE: 45
BORN: SUDBURY, ONTARIO
16 FEBRUARY 1961 TO 1 AUGUST 2010
SNC LAVALIN PAE
CANADIAN CONTRACTOR AUGMENTATION PROGRAM (CANCAP)

INTERNATIONAL SECURITY ASSISTANCE FORCE
TASK FORCE 1-10 ROTO 9
KANDAHAR - AFGHANISTAN

SNC · LAVALIN
PAE
CANCAP

AFGHANISTAN

Master Corporal Francis Roy
AGE: 31
BORN: RIMOUSKI, QUEBEC
01 NOVEMBER 1979 - 25 JUNE 2011
SPECIAL OPERATIONS TASK FORCE

SPECIAL OPERATIONS TASK FORCE
KANDAHAR - AFGHANISTAN

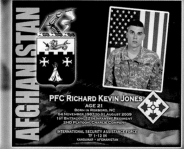

AFGHANISTAN

SENIOR AIRMAN BRADLEY R. SMITH
AGE: 24
11 SEPTEMBER 1985 - 03 JANUARY 2010
BORN IN LITTLE ROCK ARKANSAS
UNIT 10TH AIR SUPPORT OPERATIONS SQUADRON (ASOS)
ATTACHED TO 1-12 INFANTRY REGIMENT
4TH BRIGADE COMBAT TEAM
4TH INFANTRY DIVISION, FORT CARSON COLORADO

INTERNATIONAL SECURITY ASSISTANCE FORCE
OP ENDURING FREEDOM
KANDAHAR - AFGHANISTAN

AFGHANISTAN

PFC RICHARD KEVIN JONES
AGE: 21
BORN IN ROXBORO, NC
04 NOVEMBER 1987 TO 01 AUGUST 2009
1ST BATTALION, 12TH INFANTRY REGIMENT
2ND PLATOON, CHARLIE COMPANY

INTERNATIONAL SECURITY ASSISTANCE FORCE
TF 1-12 IN
KANDAHAR - AFGHANISTAN

AFGHANISTAN

SGT JAMES MICHAEL NOLEN
AGE: 25
31 MARCH 1984 TO 22 NOVEMBER 2009
BORN IN ALVIN, TEXAS
2ND BATTALION, 508TH PARACHUTE INFANTRY REGIMENT
CHARLIE COMPANY

INTERNATIONAL SECURITY ASSISTANCE FORCE
TF 2FURY
KANDAHAR - AFGHANISTAN

FURY FROM THE SKY

AIRBORNE

PFC MARCUS A. TYNES
AGE 19
BORN IN MORENO VALLEY, CALIFORNIA
21 MARCH 1990 TO 22 NOVEMBER 2009
2ND BATTALION, 508TH PARACHUTE INFANTRY REGIMENT
CHARLIE COMPANY
INTERNATIONAL SECURITY ASSISTANCE FORCE
TF 2FURY
KANDAHAR • AFGHANISTAN

SPC BRIAN ROBERT BOWMAN
AGE 24
BORN IN CRAWFORDSVILLE, INDIANA
24 JULY 1985 TO 03 JANUARY 2010
1ST BATTALION, 12TH INFANTRY REGIMENT
MEDICAL PLATOON, HEADQUARTERS AND HEADQUARTERS COMPANY
INTERNATIONAL SECURITY ASSISTANCE FORCE
TF 1-12 IN
KANDAHAR • AFGHANISTAN

SPC BOBBY JUSTIN PAGAN
AGE 25
BORN IN AUSTIN, TX
23 NOVEMBER 1984 TO 13 FEBRUARY 2010
1ST BATTALION, 12TH INFANTRY REGIMENT
2ND PLATOON, ALPHA COMPANY
INTERNATIONAL SECURITY ASSISTANCE FORCE
TF 1-12 IN
KANDAHAR • AFGHANISTAN

SSG SCOTT BRUNKHORST
AGE 25
BORN IN COLORADO
24 NOVEMBER 1984 TO 30 MARCH 2010
2ND BATTALION, 508TH PARACHUTE INFANTRY REGIMENT
CHARLIE COMPANY
INTERNATIONAL SECURITY ASSISTANCE FORCE
TF 2FURY
KANDAHAR • AFGHANISTAN

1ST LT JOSEPH J. THEINERT
AGE 24
BORN IN SAG HARBOR/SHELTER ISLAND, NY
14 FEBRUARY 1986 TO 04 JUNE 2010
1ST SQUADRON, 71ST CAVALRY REGIMENT
INTERNATIONAL SECURITY ASSISTANCE FORCE
TF 1-71
KANDAHAR • AFGHANISTAN

SGT JASON ADAM MCLEOD
AGE 22
BORN IN CRYSTAL LAKE, IL
16 SEPTEMBER 1987 TO 23 NOVEMBER 2009
704TH BRIGADE SUPPORT BATTALION
MAINTENANCE PLATOON, ECHO COMPANY
INTERNATIONAL SECURITY ASSISTANCE FORCE
TF 1-12 IN
KANDAHAR • AFGHANISTAN

SGT JOSHUA ALLEN LENGSTORF
AGE 24
BORN IN YONCALLA, OR
03 DECEMBER 1985 TO 03 JANUARY 2010
1ST BATTALION, 12TH INFANTRY REGIMENT
3RD PLATOON, BRAVO COMPANY
INTERNATIONAL SECURITY ASSISTANCE FORCE
TF 1-12 IN
KANDAHAR • AFGHANISTAN

SGT JEREMIAH THOMAS WITTMAN
AGE 26
BORN IN DARBY, MT
09 JULY 1983 TO 13 FEBRUARY 2010
1ST BATTALION, 12TH INFANTRY REGIMENT
FIRE SUPPORT ELEMENT, HEADQUARTERS AND HEADQUARTERS COMPANY
INTERNATIONAL SECURITY ASSISTANCE FORCE
TF 1-12 IN
KANDAHAR • AFGHANISTAN

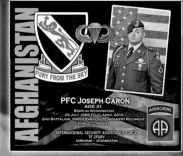

PFC JOSEPH CARON
AGE 21
BORN IN WASHINGTON
29 JULY 1988 TO 11 APRIL 2010
2ND BATTALION, 508TH PARACHUTE INFANTRY REGIMENT
CHARLIE COMPANY
INTERNATIONAL SECURITY ASSISTANCE FORCE
TF 2FURY
KANDAHAR • AFGHANISTAN

SPC BRENDAN P. NEENAN
AGE 21
BORN IN ENTERPRISE, AL
14 OCTOBER 1988 TO 07 JUNE 2010
508TH PARACHUTE INFANTRY REGIMENT
INTERNATIONAL SECURITY ASSISTANCE FORCE
TF 2FURY
KANDAHAR • AFGHANISTAN

SGT ALBERT DONO WARE
AGE 27
BORN IN MONROVIA, LIBERIA
26 NOVEMBER 1982 TO 18 DECEMBER 2009
2ND BATTALION, 508TH PARACHUTE INFANTRY REGIMENT
FOXTROT COMPANY
INTERNATIONAL SECURITY ASSISTANCE FORCE
TF 2FURY
KANDAHAR • AFGHANISTAN

CAPT PAUL PEÑA
AGE 27
BORN IN SAN MARCOS, TEXAS
08 JULY 1982 TO 19 JANUARY 2010
2ND BATTALION, 508TH PARACHUTE INFANTRY REGIMENT
ALPHA COMPANY
INTERNATIONAL SECURITY ASSISTANCE FORCE
TF 1-12 IN
KANDAHAR • AFGHANISTAN

PFC JR SALVACION
AGE 27
BORN IN EWA BEACH, HAWAII
30 DECEMBER 1982 TO 21 FEBRUARY 2010
1ST BATTALION, 12TH INFANTRY REGIMENT
2ND PLATOON, DELTA COMPANY
INTERNATIONAL SECURITY ASSISTANCE FORCE
TF 1-12 IN
KANDAHAR • AFGHANISTAN

SGT MICHAEL KEITH INGRAM JR.
AGE 23
BORN IN MONROE, MICHIGAN
6 MARCH 1987 TO 17 APRIL 2010
1ST BATTALION, 12TH INFANTRY REGIMENT
CHARLIE COMPANY
INTERNATIONAL SECURITY ASSISTANCE FORCE
TF 1-12
KANDAHAR • AFGHANISTAN

PFC BENJAMIN J. PARK
AGE 25
BORN IN FAIRFAX STATION, VA
21 JUNE 1984 TO 18 JUNE 2010
502ND INFANTRY REGIMENT
INTERNATIONAL SECURITY ASSISTANCE FORCE
TF 2 FURY
KANDAHAR • AFGHANISTAN

SENIOR AIRMAN DANIEL JAMES JOHNSON
AGE 23
BORN IN ELY, MINNESOTA (MN)
20 JUN 1972 TO 5 OCT 2010
30TH CIVIL ENGINEER SQUADRON, VANDENBERG AIR FORCE BASE
ATTACHED TO 789TH EXPLOSIVE ORDNANCE DISPOSAL UNIT (EOD)
INTERNATIONAL SECURITY ASSISTANCE FORCE
TF 1-12 IN
KANDAHAR • AFGHANISTAN

PV2 JOHN PHILLIP DION
AGE 19
BORN IN SHATTUCK, OKLAHOMA
04 FEBRUARY 1990 TO 03 JANUARY 2010
2ND BATTALION, 508TH PARACHUTE INFANTRY REGIMENT
RECONNAISSANCE PLATOON, HEADQUARTERS AND HEADQUARTERS COMPANY
INTERNATIONAL SECURITY ASSISTANCE FORCE
TF 1-12 IN
KANDAHAR • AFGHANISTAN

SFC CARLOS M. SANTOS-SILVA
AGE 32
BORN IN WIESBADEN, GERMANY
04 NOVEMBER 1977 TO 22 MARCH 2010
2ND BATTALION, 508TH PARACHUTE INFANTRY REGIMENT
CHARLIE COMPANY
INTERNATIONAL SECURITY ASSISTANCE FORCE
TF 2FURY
KANDAHAR • AFGHANISTAN

SENIOR AIRMAN MICHAEL JOHN BURAS
AGE 23
BORN IN FITZGERALD, GEORGIA (GA)
28 JUL 1987 TO 21 SEP 2010
99TH CIVIL ENGINEER SQUADRON, NELLIS AIR FORCE BASE
ATTACHED TO 703RD EXPLOSIVE ORDNANCE DISPOSAL UNIT (EOD)
INTERNATIONAL SECURITY ASSISTANCE FORCE
TF 1-71
KANDAHAR • AFGHANISTAN

STAFF SGT EDWARDO LOREDO
AGE 34
BORN IN HOUSTON, TX
25 JUNE 1975 TO 24 JUNE 2010
508TH PARACHUTE INFANTRY REGIMENT
INTERNATIONAL SECURITY ASSISTANCE FORCE
TF 1 FURY
KANDAHAR • AFGHANISTAN

STAFF SGT CHRISTOPHER F. CABACOY
AGE 30
BORN IN VIRGINIA BEACH, VA
14 AUGUST 1979 TO 05 JULY 2010
1ST SQUADRON, 71ST CAVALRY REGIMENT

INTERNATIONAL SECURITY ASSISTANCE FORCE
TF 1-71
KANDAHAR - AFGHANISTAN

1ST LT CHRISTOPHER S. GOEKE
AGE 23
BORN IN CLEVELAND, OH
18 AUGUST 1986 TO 13 JULY 2010
508TH PARACHUTE INFANTRY REGIMENT

INTERNATIONAL SECURITY ASSISTANCE FORCE
TF 1 FURY
KANDAHAR - AFGHANISTAN

SPC JASON JOHNSTON
AGE 24
BORN IN ROCHESTER, NEW YORK
10 DECEMBER 1985 TO 26 DECEMBER 2009
2ND BATTALION, 508TH PARACHUTE INFANTRY REGIMENT
BRAVO COMPANY

INTERNATIONAL SECURITY ASSISTANCE FORCE
TF 2FURY
KANDAHAR - AFGHANISTAN

PFC EDWIN C. WOOD
AGE 18
BORN IN OMAHA, NE
28 AUGUST 1991 TO 05 JULY 2010
1ST SQUADRON, 71ST CAVALRY REGIMENT

INTERNATIONAL SECURITY ASSISTANCE FORCE
TF 1-71
KANDAHAR - AFGHANISTAN

STAFF SGT CHRISTOPHER T. STOUT
AGE 34
BORN IN JEFFERSON COUNTY, KY
01 JANUARY 1976 TO 13 JULY 2010
508TH PARACHUTE INFANTRY REGIMENT

INTERNATIONAL SECURITY ASSISTANCE FORCE
TF 1 FURY
KANDAHAR - AFGHANISTAN

SGT 1ST CLASS CHARLES M. SADELL
AGE 34
BORN IN COLUMBIA, MISSOURI
11 OCT 1976 TO 24 OCT 2010
1ST SQUADRON, 71ST CAVALRY REGIMENT
HHT, S2 SECTION

INTERNATIONAL SECURITY ASSISTANCE FORCE
TF 1-71
KANDAHAR - AFGHANISTAN

STAFF SGT JESSE W. AINSWORTH
AGE 24
BORN IN BAYTOWN, TX
17 SEPTEMBER 1985 TO 10 JULY 2010
1ST SQUADRON, 71ST CAVALRY REGIMENT

INTERNATIONAL SECURITY ASSISTANCE FORCE
TF 1-71
KANDAHAR - AFGHANISTAN

STAFF SGT SHELDON L. TATE
AGE 27
BORN IN HINESVILLE, GA
8 SEPTEMBER 1982 TO 13 JULY 2010
508TH PARACHUTE INFANTRY REGIMENT

INTERNATIONAL SECURITY ASSISTANCE FORCE
TF 1 FURY
KANDAHAR - AFGHANISTAN

SGT MICHAEL F. PARANZIO
AGE: 22
BORN IN MIDDLETOWN, RHODE ISLAND
4 DEC 1987 TO 5 NOV 2010
1ST SQUADRON, 71ST CAVALRY REGIMENT
B TROOP, 1ST PLATOON

INTERNATIONAL SECURITY ASSISTANCE FORCE
TF 1-71
KANDAHAR - AFGHANISTAN

SGT DONALD R. EDGERTON
AGE 33
BORN IN MOBILE, AL
09 JULY 1977 TO 10 JULY 2010
1ST SQUADRON, 71ST CAVALRY REGIMENT

INTERNATIONAL SECURITY ASSISTANCE FORCE
TF 1-71
KANDAHAR - AFGHANISTAN

TSGT ADAM K. GINETT
AGE 29
BORN IN KNIGHTDALE, NORTH CAROLINA
3 MAY 1980 TO 19 JANUARY 2010
755TH AIR EXPEDITIONARY SQUADRON BRAVO FLIGHT EOD TM 6
ATTACHED TO ALPHA COMPANY 2ND BATTALION, 508TH
PARACHUTE INFANTRY REGIMENT

INTERNATIONAL SECURITY ASSISTANCE FORCE
TF 2FURY
KANDAHAR - AFGHANISTAN

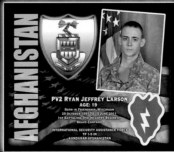

PV2 RYAN JEFFREY LARSON
AGE: 19
BORN IN FRIENDSHIP, WISCONSIN
29 OCTOBER 1991 TO 15 JUNE 2011
1ST BATTALION, 5TH INFANTRY REGIMENT
BRAVO COMPANY

INTERNATIONAL SECURITY ASSISTANCE FORCE
TF 1-5 IN
KANDAHAR AFGHANISTAN

COMMANDERS & ROTATIONS

Op ATHENA – KANDAHAR

BGen D.A. Fraser	2006
BGen T.J Grant	2006 - 2007
BGen J.R.M.G. Laroche	2007 - 2008
BGen D.W. Thompson	2008 - 2009
BGen J.H. Vance	2009
BGen J.B.G. Menard	2009 - 2010
BGen J.H. Vance	2010
BGen D.J Milner	2010 - 2011
BGen C.A. Lamarre	2011

Op ATHENA – KABUL

Col M.D. Hodgson	Roto 0	2003 - 2004
Col J.R.A. Tremblay	Roto 1	2004
Col W.J. Ellis	Roto 2	2004 - 2005
Col W. Semianiw	Roto 3	2005
Col S.P. Noonan	Roto 4	2005 - 2006

ISAF Commanders

BGen P.J Devlin	Commd MN Brigade	2003 - 2004
Col J.P.P.J. LaCroix	Commd MN Brigade	2004 - 2004
LGen R.J. Hillier	Commd ISAF	2004
BGen A.B Leslie	DComd ISAF	2003 - 2004

Op ATTENTION Commanders – Kandahar

MGen S. Beare	2010 - 2011
MGen M. Day	2011 - 2012
MGen J.R. Ferron	2012 - 2013
MGen D.J. Milner	2013 - 2014

COYOTE
Armoured
Reconnaissance
Vehicle

COUGAR
Explosive
Ordnance
Recovery
Vehicle

LAV III
Light
Armoured
Vehicle

G-WAGON
Light
Utility
Vehicle
Wheeled

TAURUS ARV
Armoured
Recovery
Vehicle

58

CANADIAN OPERATIONAL AREAS
AFGHANISTAN

Summary of Abbreviations

ANA	Afghan National Army
ANP	Afghanistan National Police
BDR	Bombardier *(Rank - Artillery Corporal)*
BG	Battle Group
CAPT	Captain *(Rank)*
CDS	Chief of the Defence Staff *(Appointment)*
CEFCOM	Canadian Expeditionary Force Command
CER	Combat Engineer Regiment
CF	Canadian Forces
CFB	Canadian Forces Base
CIMIC	Civil-Military Cooperation
CJOC	Canadian Joint Operations Command
COIN	Counterinsurgency Academy
CO	Commanding Officer *(Appt)*
COL	Colonel *(Rank)*
COY	Company
CPL	Corporal *(Rank)*
CMTC	Canadian Manoeuvre Training Center
CTF	Coalition Task Force
CWO	Chief Warrant Officer *(Rank)*
DCO	Deputy Commanding Officer aka 2 i/c *(Appointment)*
DND	Department of National Defence *(Canada)*
EOD	Explosive Ordnance Disposal
EXCON	Exercise Control Center
FOB	Forward Operating Base
Gen	General *(Rank)*
GNR	Gunner *(Rank - Artillery Private)*
HMCS	Her Majesty's Canadian Ship
HQ	Headquarters
IED	Improvised Explosive Device
IRF(L)	Immediate Reaction Force *(Land)*
ISAF	International Security Assistance Force
JTF-2	Joint Task Force 2 - *Canada's Special Forces*
KAF	Kandahar Air Field
KPRT	Kandahar Provincial Reconstruction Team
LAV	Light Armoured Vehicle
LCol	Lieutenant Colonel *(Rank)*
LGen	Lieutenant General *(Rank)*
LdSH (RC)	Lord Strathcona's Horse (Royal Canadians)
LT	Lieutenant *(Rank)* - *pronounced Leftenant*
MAJ	Major *(Rank)*
MCpl	Master Corporal *(Rank)*
MGen	Major General *(Rank)*
MWO	Master Warrant Officer *(Rank)*

NDHQ	National Defence Headquarters – Ottawa
NATO	North Atlantic Treaty Organization
OC	Officer Commanding *(Appointment)*
OMLT	Operational Mentoring Liaison Team
Op	Abbreviation for Operation
PL	Platoon
PO	Petty Officer *(Navy rank)*
PPCLI	Princess Patricia's Canadian Light Infantry *(3 Battalions)*
PRT	Provincial Reconstruction Team
PTE	Private *(Rank)*
R22eR	Royal 22nd Regiment aka The VanDoos *(3 Battalions)*
RCHA	Royal Canadian Horse Artillery Regular Force - *(3 Regiments)*
RCA	Royal Regiment of Canadian Artillery
RCD	Royal Canadian Dragoons
RCR	The Royal Canadian Regiment *(3 Battalions)*
RPG	Rocket Propelled Grenade
RSM	Regimental Sergeant Major *(Appointment)*
SGT	Sergeant *(Rank)*
SPR	Sapper *(Rank – Engineers Private)*
SQN	Squadron
SVC BN	Service Battalion
12 RBC	12th Régiment blindé du Canada
2 I/C	Second in Command *(Appt)*
TF	Task Force
TP	Troop
TPR	Trooper *(Rank – Armoured Private)*
UN	United Nations
Van Doos	Royal 22nd Regiment
WO	Warrant Officer *(Rank)*
WES	Weapons Effects Simulation

PHOTO CREDITS

The vast majority of the photos in this book were taken by members of Canadian Armed Forces Combat Camera, a dedicated assembly of highly skilled photographers, Public Affairs Officers and civilian support staff.

Since 1990, they have braved the elements, dangled from helicopters, taken flak from soldiers in the heat of battle, dodged a few bullets and bombs- all to get the 'right' shot.

MCpl Shilo Adamson, a seasoned 'CC' photographer with a keen eye (and a great smile) has been with us on this project from the outset. Countless hours of her own time were spent on photo selection and the research on photo credits. She deserves a very special thank-you for a job well done.

The author would also like to offer sincere condolences to the family, and colleagues of Master Corporal D.J. Priede. A native of Burlington Ontario. Darrel lost his life on 31 May 2007 in the line of duty, doing what he did best - while serving his country.

Note: All CAF Combat Camera photos are © DND

ACKNOWLEDGMENTS

This book is truly a massive collaboration that has taken many years to assemble. I am honoured and humbled to have been in a position to gather the many pieces involved - and put them into a framework through which the average Canadian can gain a clear understanding of what our Canadian Armed Forces have contributed to their continued freedom and security.

There is no way that I can thank everyone who has contributed to this tome, so I will just have to do my best to acknowledge those most obvious and accept the inevitability that I will unfortunately miss someone key and dear. To you, please accept my profound apology.

First of all, I'd like to extend my sincere appreciation to **LGen Stu Beare**, a man of vision and a great leader. Recognizing the need for a book of this nature, he and his staff of stalwarts including: **Command CWO Serge Froment, LCol Rob Foster, LCol Dyrald Cross, LCol Christian Lemay, Cory Hunter, Capt Indira Thackorie** and **MCpl Shilo Adamson** have all cooperated to the fullest.

Norman Leach, my editor, my rock! A man with unending patience, solid work ethic, dogged determination and the ability to convert complicated facts into readable matter. To **Margaret McGirr**, my Grade 5 teacher who recognized some degree of artistic ability and sent me off to Saturday morning art school. To **Dave Leeson**, my first real *army buddy* who showed me how to properly apply and fasten my puttees, back in 1961 - and to **Capt (Ret) Steve Pura**, **CWO Dave Holberton** who both set a great examples of military bearing, personal dedication and leadership!

A very special thanks to my lifelong friend, confidant and mentor, **BGen (Ret) Vic Lanctis** who was very engaged in the editing process – both in French and English…and to **Major Joe Nunez**, for his encouragement and connection to **Capt Michel David**, of the famed *Van Doo's* - the Godsend from Montreal who bailed us at the eleventh hour to translate the entire book to French.

Everyone needs a go-to-guy. **Lt.Terry Larson** is one of those people. Being a bit of a *scrounger* (a compliment in military terms), Terry returned from theatre with an array of *unclassified* but highly detailed maps and reference materials of KAF that were very helpful in providing me with an accurate image of camp facilities - and their relative locations.

In the interest of accuracy, and for those of you who may be sticklers for detail, we decided to use the old moniker CF throughout the book (vice CAF), because that change in nomenclature was only announced in March 2013 – effectively after our time in Afghanistan.

To those of you in uniform – and the supportive families behind every serving member of our military, police and first responders - I salute your courage and dedication to making Canada a safe country in which to live. All Canadians who enjoy the right and priviledges of living in such a great country, owe you a debt of gratitude for the safety and security you bring to our lives.

You are the kind of people who make Canada a great country in which to live.

To the families of those who gave their lives in the service of Canada, many of whom I have met and established a friendship, my heart goes our to each and every one of you. Know that the people of Canada feel your pain and share in your loss.

And finally **to each of you**, the unmentioned that have touched my life in some way over the years - please accept my gratitude for giving me the tools and life experiences necessary to turn this book into something tangible.

Following is a list of people, in no particular order, who have contributed to the research, fact finding, coaching, mentoring and helping to make it all come together. This book would not be a reality without their help.

LCol (Ret) Ross Nairne
BGen (Ret) Ray Romses
Major (Ret) Bruce Henwood
LCol (Ret) Bill Schultz
LCol Tod Strickland
LCol (Ret) Tom Bradley
MGen (Ret) Tim Grant
LCol (Ret) Bruce Bolton
Major (Ret) Justin McNeill
BGen (Ret) Barry Ashton
Chuck Stormes
Major (Ret) Bill Hampson
LCol John Cochrane
Grady McLeod
Iain McLeod
WO Wayne Edwards
LCol (Ret) Grant McLean
Dr. George Vanderburgh
CWO Rick Day
CWO Alain Bergeron
Major Jim Fisher
CWO Dave Mahon
Lane Kranenburg
Irene Lythall
Heather LeDrew
Cst. Eric Lehaney
WO Ed Storey
LCol (Ret) Randy Hallett
Capt Patrick Lottinville
Rauri Nicholson
D/M Ed Luikaitis
Francois Arseneault
Cpl Lizanne Guay
Capt (Ret) AJ (Jim) Fisk
Earl Brown, Esq.
Major Jason King
Cpl Tina Gillies
...and the enduring spirit of my good friend and travelling companion **N. Guthrie Woods!**

The writing and subsequent publication of this book was inspired by a weekend in 2008 - spent with a group of writers and publishers in the northern BC community of

Organized and facilitated by Fort Nelson writer/publisher Earl Brown, Dan Poynter, world renowned author, speaker and prolific self-publisher encouraged a group of up and coming authors to write a book.....so here is mine!

Rod A. McLeod
Author & Designer

SHELLDRAKE PUBLISHING CO., LTD.
Copyright © Rod A. McLeod, 2014

Editor: Norman Leach
Design: Rod A.McLeod
Printer: Friesen Press
Printed in Canada

Library and Archives Canada Cataloguing in Publication

McLeod, Rod A.
      VIGIL, Canada's Sacrifice in Afghanistan/ Rod A. McLeod

ISBN 978-9937353-0-1
1. Canadian Army - Afghanistan, 2 War - Canada - Afghanistan 2012 - 2014.

First edition - 1 August 2014

Also by this author - **Iain MacCrimmon's Book II Music for the Great Highland Bagpipe**
co-authored and published by Iain MacCrimmon and Rod A. McLeod 1978 - Calgary

COINS...AND THE MILITARY!

During the first Great War, a moderately wealthy American flying officer had a series of coins minted, bearing the squadron badge. He gifted them to his fellow officers to promote unit loyalty and esprit-de-corps. As the war progressed, one of his comrades was shot down over enemy territory.

He managed to find some civilian clothing and was in the process of making his way back to friendly territory when he was challenged by the local underground movement - and was at risk of being identified as a spy. The only way he could substantiate his loyalty was by presenting his squadron coin which he kept in a leather pouch about his neck. Since then, this tradition has been embraced by the military as a way to prove membership, promote camaraderie and demonstrate unit pride.

Recognized as a welcome *Americanism*, the use of challenge coins is relatively new to the Canadian Forces. General (Ret) Rick Hillier, having spent several years in key command positions with the American army, recognized the benefits of using coins and promoted their use as the Canadians began to train and work with the US military in preparation for Afghanistan.

While many organizations use coins for award or presentation purposes, many still respect the time honoured tradition of *challenging* a comrade to see if they are carrying their coin. If not, the challenged individual may be expected to pay for a libation. On the other hand, if he does present his coin, the challenger is obligated to pay for the round.

AFPP-International is a Calgary based company specializing in the design and production of coins and award products specifically for the military. During the war in Afghanistan, the company created and provided several thousand coins for the CF – many of which are displayed on the end papers and pages of this book. As you 'had to be there' in order to get one, these coins have become highly collectible.

The most popular coin, used by a succession of Task Force Commanders, features a Mullah's head on the obverse (front) side. It was first introduced by BGen Tim Grant and was subsequently used by the next nine consecutive commanders.

Shelldrake Publishing Co., Ltd. and AFPP-International are offering a numbered series of beautifully minted coins made of die struck cartridge brass and finished in 24k gold plate. Net proceeds resulting from the sale of this coin will be given to the Support Our Troops campaign to help the members and families deal with issues of post traumatic stress and injuries sustained – both visible and invisible - as a result of military service.

For more information on acquiring this coin, please visit the Vigil web page at:

www.vigilbook.ca